Contents

Unit 1 Love life!

1 The West Street five ▸ pp. 6–7

a) *Read pp. 6–7 in your student's book again. Are the statements below true or false? Mark a letter.*

		True	False
1	Bex would like to go out with Ed.	P	Y
2	Peanut hasn't got a girlfriend.	H	K
3	Minty always tries hard to look good.	A	I
4	Peanut and Ed have known each other a long time.	L	M
5	Bex doesn't care much about clothes and make-up.	I	I
6	Minty is sometimes bossy.	P	T
7	Bex is Toby's girlfriend.	N	N
8	Minty is very much like her brother.	T	U
9	Peanut is interested in all kinds of things and he knows a lot.	T	U
10	Peanut is a bit shy but people like him.	T	P

If your answers are correct, the letters give you the name of a West Street character: ____________

b) *Think about how the West Street story might continue. Choose one character and write a few sentences about what might happen to this person in the next episode.*

I think … and … would interest me most …

____

____

____

2 Choose a friend ▸ p. 7

Which boy and which girl of the West Street five would you choose to be your friends? Say what you think is positive about them and why. Write a few sentences in your exercise book.

I think I would choose … and … to be my friends because …

3 Extra Teen drama series ▸ p. 7

Do you like teen drama series on German TV? Why do you think they are popular? What is special about them? What kind of problems do the teenagers often have? Answer the questions in a paragraph. Write in your exercise book.

I really like/don't like teen drama series.
They are very popular because …
The teenagers in the series often …
This is interesting/boring because …

4 Jeff's problem

▸ p. 9 • WB (pp. 68–69)

Read about Jeff's problem. What advice would you give him? Write your ideas in your exercise book (about 60–80 words).

Jeff could ... *If I were Jeff, I would ...* *I think Jeff should ...* *perhaps Katie can ...*

Dear mag,
My name's Jeff and I have this problem:
I was with Katie, a girl from my school, for a year. It was a good relationship. Then her dad got a job in South America, so they moved there. At first we kept in touch by phone and computer, but I didn't like being alone. Katie didn't know when they would be back in the UK. After a few months I started going out with another girl, Ella, also from our school, and communication with Katie became less and less.
Now, after a year and a half in Brazil, Katie and her family have returned unexpectedly, and she is back at our school – in the same class as Ella.
I don't know what to do. I think about Katie more and more. When I see her I just feel the same as always when we were together. I'm still with Ella, so I know this isn't fair. But what can I do? The relationship with Katie was never really over. It was just the miles between us.
I don't know how Katie feels. We haven't really talked. It's difficult. I expect she knows about Ella - they are in the same class. I hate this situation. I really need to know if Katie has another boyfriend or if she wants me back. Do we have a second chance? What should I do?

5 WORDS Personal qualities

▸ p. 10

a) *Write the words in two lists: positive and negative.*

ambitious • *arrogant* • boring • bossy • confident • easy-going • funny • hard-working • honest • horrible • jealous • lazy • likeable • relaxed • reliable • rude • unfair • useless

☺ *ambitious,* ______________________________

____

____

☹ *arrogant,* ______________________________

____

____

b) *Add at least three more words to each list in a).*

c) *Complete the sentences about yourself. Use words from above.*

I always try to be ______________________________

I know that I'm sometimes ______________________________

0305 I hope I'm never ______________________________

Now you

Which positive qualities are important for you in a best friend? Which negative qualities are in your opinion the worst? Why? Use the words in exercise 5 and your own words. Write a few sentences.

For me it's important that a friend is ...   *I don't like people who ...*

6 Band night (Simple present and progressive) ▸ p. 10 • WB (p. 70)

Tim is describing a photo which he's sending to an e-friend. Here's part of his e-mail. Underline the correct form in brackets. The words in bold can help you.

1 I ('m sending/send) you a photo of me with my band.

2 **In the photo** we ('re rehearsing/rehearse) at the youth club. There's a local band competition in two weeks. We're pretty good and we (want/are wanting) to win.

3 We **usually** (are practising/practise) once a week, but **this week** we ('re practising/practise) more. We **always** (write/'re writing) our own songs, of course. **At the moment** we ('re writing/write) our first album, and we (work/'re working) really hard on it **just now**.

4 So who's who in the picture? Well, the guy on drums is Brad. He (knows/is knowing) a lot about sound recording, and he's a pretty cool drummer.

5 The boy who ('s wearing/wears) the orange shirt **in the photo** is Dave. And I'm the guy in the middle.

6 The girl on the right is Fran, my girlfriend. **Usually** she (is singing/sings) and she (plays/is playing) the guitar, but **in the photo** she (is practising/practises) a new song. She (is wanting/wants) to be a nurse – if we (don't become/aren't becoming) rich and famous with our band (joke!).

0406
0407
0408

7 EVERYDAY ENGLISH SPEAKING
Keeping a conversation going ▸ p. 11 • WB (pp. 67–68)

a) What is important if you want to keep a conversation going? Find the right words to complete these statements:

Find out the person's ______________ mean , where he/she lives, etc.

Make a few ______________ plmitcnomes .

Make ______________ momtnesc that show you are interested.

Find out about the person's likes and ______________ strintese .

Ask ______________ sutiqenso with when, where, what, etc.

b) Dale would like to get to know Judy. How could he keep Judy interested in the conversation? Circle A or B.

Dale Hi, I'm Dale.
Judy Hi.
Dale (A): Sorry, what was your name?
B: Er ..., and who are you?
Judy I'm Judy.
Dale A: Oh. OK. Well, I'm 16 and I live in ...
B: Oh, that's a nice name. Do you live around here?
Judy Yes, but actually we're new in town.
Dale A: I thought I hadn't seen you here before. Where are you from?
B: Oh, er ... I see.
Judy We moved here from Liverpool just three weeks ago.
Dale: A: I don't think I've been there. Maybe when I was a kid.
B: Liverpool. Right! I've been there. Now that is a great place – for music too.
Judy That's true. We have some great clubs.
Dale A: What kind of music are you into?
B: Good.
Judy R&B mainly. Some Dance-pop too.
Dale A: Oh, so you like Rihanna and Beyoncé. Cool. Me too. And what about films?
B: Oh, my last girlfriend liked R&B too.

c) Write questions which you could use to keep a conversation going. Ideas: ***music, films, TV, sports, travel, school, free time, after-school jobs.***

What kind of music do you like? Which sports do you do?

____

____

____

____

d) Write an interesting conversation between Jack and Josie, UK teenagers. Use the conversation skills that you have practised in a)–c).
Write down some useful phrases, prepare some topics to talk about, think of useful questions.
Write in your exercise book. Prepare to act out your dialogue in class with a partner.

'B, pp. 9–51

8 Two film reviews ▸ p. 12

Read the film reviews on page 12 of your student's book again. Which statements match the two films? Write numbers 2–8 under the film titles.

Bend it like Beckham	Twilight
1,	

1 This very funny film is set in the UK.
2 The teenage girl in this film has just moved to a new school.
3 The soundtrack has British and Indian music.
4 This film is a fantasy drama.
5 The film shows problems of living in two very different cultures.
6 The special effects in this film are brilliant.
7 Getting pregnant is not the greatest danger in this relationship.
8 Problems between parents and children are also a topic in this film.

9 LISTENING A radio phone-in ▸ p. 14 • WB (p. 66) 2

Test

Four young people talk about their problems on a radio phone-in. Before you listen, read the advice (statements 1–6 below). Then listen to the problems and choose the advice which fits each problem best. Write a number after each name. Two pieces of advice do not fit any of the problems.

Beth: ☐ • Matthew: ☐ • Simon: ☐ • Lauren: ☐

1 You don't seem to be happy. This girl is slowly killing your relationship, so end it yourself.
2 It may be just a flirt, it may be more. But if he has a girlfriend, keep away.
3 Don't break up a friendship for a relationship that probably won't last anyway. Both of you should dump this guy.
4 You want this boy as a boyfriend, not just a mate. But you can't make this happen. For the moment just enjoy his friendship and give it time.
5 Maybe he likes you too, but he's too shy to talk to you when you're in a group. Try to be alone with him and start a conversation. Then just see how it goes.
6 Maybe you should tell your girlfriend about your problem. You won't lose her if your relationship is as good as you say. Secret feelings are often not as strong when you talk about them, and maybe the new girl has a boyfriend anyway.

WB, pp. 44–48

0609

10 READING Dive

▸ p. 14 • WB (pp. 66–67)

a) Look at the pictures. What do you think the text may be about? Write a few sentences.

The pictures show … *Maybe the girl …* *It looks as if …*

b) Look at the text quickly. What kind of text is it? Tick a box.

A book review. ☐ An online blog. ☐ A TV film review. ☐

Dive ★★★★★

The TV drama *Dive*[1] (2010) was written and directed by TV author Dominic Savage. It tells the story of Lindsey (young star Aisling Loftus), a 16-year-old schoolgirl who is training hard to be part of the British diving[2] team at the London 2012 Olympics. Everything is fine until Lindsey's father leaves home suddenly and her mother's new boyfriend moves in. Lindsey is upset. Out of protest she misses her diving training and hangs out in the park with some beer-drinking classmates, something she has never done before. But this one time changes Lindsey's life and her dream – she gets pregnant. The father is Robert (Jack O'Connell), an arrogant but popular boy, who Lindsey doesn't know well.

The film shows how Lindsey and her boyfriend try to live with the new situation. Robert's father is angry. Lindsey decides to give up her Olympic dream and have the baby. The teenagers argue and break up, but they come together again before the birth. Living together is difficult, but the young parents grow in their new roles. Lindsey begins her daily diving training again. The young father watches with the baby.

This is not a typical story of broken homes and lost dreams. It is realistic, but optimistic. It is brilliantly acted and beautifully filmed. On the negative side, the violin soundtrack is used too much.

Although *Dive* is about a teenage pregnancy, it is a story for everybody.

c) Now read the text carefully and tick the correct statements.

In the review the reader is informed about …

1 what kind of film it is. ✔
2 who wrote and directed the film. ☐
3 where the action takes place. ☐
4 the year the film was made. ☐
5 what the film is about. ☐
6 who the main actors are. ☐
7 the supporting actors[3] and their roles. ☐
8 the quality of the actors. ☐
9 how the film ends. ☐
10 how much the film cost to make. ☐
11 the soundtrack. ☐
12 special effects. ☐
13 who will like the film. ☐
14 what other films the main actors have made. ☐

'B, pp. 5–59
0710

[1]dive ['daɪv] *Kopfsprung* [2]diving ['daɪvɪŋ] *Turmspringen* [3]supporting actor *Nebendarsteller/in*

11 WORDS Film words ▸ p. 14

a) Write the film words in two lists: kind of film and words to describe a film.

action • adventure • amazing • awful • cartoon • clever • comedy • crime drama • funny • horror • musical • police drama • realistic • romantic sad • scary • science fiction • silly • stupid • terrible • thriller • western

Different kinds of films:

action, ______

______

We can describe films as:

amazing, ______

______

b) What kind of films do you like best, and why? What kind of films don't you like, and why? Write two sentences. Use words from both lists.

I really like/I never watch ... because they're usually ... and ...

1 ______

______

2 ______

______

0811

12 WRITING A film I really enjoyed ▸ p. 14 • WB (pp. 68–69)

Test

Think of a film that you really enjoyed. Write a review about it. Look at workbook exercises 8 and 10 and the reviews in your student's book on pp. 12–13 for ideas. In your review, mention the following:

- the film's title
- the kind of film it is (comedy, cartoon film etc.)
- where and when the action takes place (country or town, past, present or future)
- names of the main actors
- the story (main events)
- the main characters (appearance, personal qualities, age)
- soundtrack or special effects
- who will like the film (teenagers, adults, kids)
- your personal opinion: what makes the film special, what you liked best

Use present tenses. Write in your exercise book. The phrases below will help you.

A film that I really enjoyed is (title) ...
It's a comedy/drama/cartoon film and it was directed by ...
It stars ...
The film tells the story of ...
At the beginning/Later/At the end ...
My favourite scene/part is when/where ...

My favourite character is ... because ...
There's a happy ending when/because ...
The acting/soundtrack/photography/dialogue is brilliant ...
The plot is clever, exciting, realistic ...
To sum up, I love this film because ...
I'd give it ... stars out of five ...

WB, pp. 52–55

13 SPEAKING Describing a picture

▸ p. 14 • SF (pp. 125–126) • WB (pp. 67–68)

a) Describe the picture. Say what you think is happening. How do you think the girl in the foreground is feeling? Make notes in your exercise book and prepare to talk about the picture in class. The words in the boxes will help you.

in the foreground/background/ middle • on the right/left • not far from • behind

dump someone • be/feel/look happy/relaxed • be/feel/look unhappy/sad/hurt/angry/shocked/ disappointed/upset/jealous

b) Prepare spoken answers to these questions:

1 How much of your free time do you spend with a boyfriend/girlfriend?
2 Where do you go with your boyfriend/girlfriend in your free time? (cinema, shopping, sport, etc.)
3 Do you think it's important to have the same interests as your boyfriend/girlfriend?

'B, pp.)–51

sometimes • usually • go out twice a week • at weekends • In my opinion, … • I (don't) think that …

14 Nina and Tim (Simple past and progressive)

▸ p. 15 • WB (pp. 70–71)

Complete what Nina says about her boyfriend Tim. Choose the correct form from the box.

wanted • was waiting (2x) • were standing • thought • tried • didn't answer • was raining • was coming • was standing • said • called

Tim is a really great boyfriend. He's so relaxed and funny. But he isn't always reliable. Last Friday we *wanted* to see the new Matt Damon action film. I'm usually early for a date, so at 7.20 I ______ for Tim outside the cinema. Lots of people ______ in the ticket queue. It ______ too, so everybody was wet. I ______ to call Tim on his mobile, but he ______.

I ______ perhaps he ______ by car and was in a traffic jam. Then, a few minutes later, he ______ me. He ______ he ______ outside the *Odeon* – with cold feet. He ______ for me! But the film was on at the *Apollo*!

Typical Tim!

0914

15 MEDIATION 17 Again

▸ p. 15 • WB (pp. 69–70)

Test

Read the summary of the 2009 teen comedy 17 Again. *Explain to a German friend, whose English isn't as good as yours, what the film is about. Don't translate into German. Give only the most important events.*

In this teen comedy Mike O'Donnell (Zac Efron) is 17 and is the star of his high school basketball team. He is sure he will get a college scholarship[1], so his future looks good. Then he discovers that his girlfriend Scarlet is pregnant. This changes his life and his future. He gives up his college plans and marries his girlfriend. Twenty years later his wife wants to divorce him, his two kids hate him and he is unsuccessful in his job. He lives with his best friend Ned. Unhappy with his life, Mike starts thinking 'what if…?' and wishes he could live his life again. Mysteriously[2], he gets the chance to be seventeen again, and suddenly he finds himself in high school - with his kids.

WB, pp. 60–61

1015

16 WRITING Boy meets girl

▸ p. 15 • WB (pp. 68–69)

Test

Look at the pictures. Then write a story in full sentences. You can use the phrases below and your own ideas. Write the story in your exercise book. Use the **simple past** *(e.g.* **went**, **showed***) and the* **past progressive** *(e.g.* **was looking***) and direct speech to make your story more interesting. Add an ending.*

1

boy – go into crowded pizza restaurant – waiter – show table near window – girl sit alone at next table – read magazine

2

girl – order salami pizza – boy – order pizza with ham and mushrooms

3

waiter – bring pizzas – wrong – look surprised – turn round – look at pizzas on other table – look at each other

4

like each other – sit together – talk excitedly

WB, pp. 52–55

[1]scholarship ['skɒləʃɪp] *Stipendium* [2]mysteriously [mɪ'stɪəriəsli] *auf geheimnisvolle Weise, unerklärlicherweise*

17 Extra WORKING WITH THE TEXT The Absolutely True Diary of a ...

▸ pp. 16–19 • WB (pp. 66–67)

a) Read pp. 16–19 in your student's book again and match the sentence halves. Write the correct letter in the box.

1 Everybody at Reardan High was shocked that ...	e	a	do something big and important.
2 Arnold thinks Penelope is dating him because ...		b	he's a rich, white boy from Reardan.
3 Penelope's father thinks she's dating Arnold because ...		c	visit lots of different countries.
4 Penelope hates living in Reardan because ...		d	she is bored and wants to do something crazy.
5 Penelope and Arnold have a dream. They want to ...		e	Penelope chose Arnold to be her friend.
6 Penelope wants to leave Reardan and ...		f	she wants to annoy him.
7 Penelope's father likes Roger because ...		g	how poor he is.
8 Arnold doesn't want to go to the diner because ...		h	everything about it is small.
9 Arnold doesn't want his classmates to know ...		i	he has no money to pay for the food.

b) Answer the questions on the text in a few sentences each.

1 L. 3 of the text says that Arnold makes a 'brave decision'. What is his decision and why is it brave?

2 Why do you think Penelope likes Arnold?

3 Describe the 'big dreams' that Arnold and Penelope have.

4 Do you think Arnold is a likeable person? Do you think you would like Arnold to be your friend too? Say why or why not.

1118
1119

Exam Check

LISTENING

1 LISTENING Friends on the net 3

a) You are going to hear five teenagers who talk about friends on the internet. First read the statements below. Listen and choose the correct statement for each person. While you are listening, write the correct letters in the boxes.

Richard: ☐ Angie: ☐ Robin: ☐

Lisa: ☐ Josie: ☐

A You can practise languages and learn about other cultures on the internet.
B The internet is the best way to make lots of new friends.
C When you sit at the computer alone, you don't make real friends because you can't speak to people.
D You can lose friends if you spend too much time on the net.
E You can find friends with exactly the same interests as you.

b) Listen again and check your answers.

LISTENING

2 LISTENING Voicemail messages 4

Robert has four voicemail messages. First read the statements below. Then listen to the messages and tick the correct box.

	True	False	Not given
Message 1			
1 If Rob joins his friends, there will be five of them.	☐	☐	☐
2 The film starts at eight o'clock.	☐	☐	☐
3 The *Odeon* cinema is Rob's favourite cinema.	☐	☐	☐
Message 2			
4 Becca has lost her mobile.	☐	☐	☐
5 Sandy and Becca wanted to go to a concert.	☐	☐	☐
6 Becca can call Sandy on 02072877355.	☐	☐	☐
Message 3			
7 Jay and Rob play in a band.	☐	☐	☐
8 Jay wants to change the next band meeting to Wednesday.	☐	☐	☐
9 It's Adam's birthday on Tuesday.	☐	☐	☐
Message 4			
10 Melinda needs help with her computer.	☐	☐	☐
11 There is a repair shop in the neighbourhood.	☐	☐	☐
12 Melinda's number is 07760049872.	☐	☐	☐

3 LISTENING Talking about free time 5

a) First read the statements about Trish, Fran, Scott and Todd (1–12).

1 Trish likes Kylie Minogue and ______________ music.

2 Trish likes to watch *Neighbours*, which is on TV on weekdays at ______________.

3 The soap has been on TV for about ______________ years.

4 Fran's ______________ watches *Neighbours* too.

5 The soap *Home and Away* is on network Seven at ______________ every day.

6 Fran's ______________ watches *Home and Away*.

7 Scott watches Aussie rules and ______________ on TV.

8 Todd only watches ______________ on TV.

9 Todd really likes ______________ sports.

10 He goes ______________ twice a week, on Mondays and Thursdays.

11 Todd asks Scott to join him at the club on ______________ after work.

12 Scott says he could get the ______________ bus.

b) Now listen to the teenagers' conversation (5). While you are listening, complete the statements in a).

c) Listen again and check your answers.

4 SPEAKING Dumped

Describe the picture. Make notes and talk for about two minutes. You can record what you say.

1 What has happened?

____

____

2 How do you think the girl is feeling?

____

____

3 What do you think the girl should do?

____

____

4 Do you think it's OK to end a friendship by text message?

____

____

SPEAKING

5 SPEAKING A cartoon

Talk about the cartoon for about three minutes. The questions in the box below will help you. Make notes first.

"YOUR MOTHER AND I FOUND OUT YOU'VE BEEN BLOGGING. WE DON'T KNOW WHAT THAT MEANS, BUT WE'D LIKE YOU TO STOP."

What can you see? • What is happening? • What does the father think of his son? • What does the son think of his father? • What is the cartoon's message? • Do you agree with what the cartoon artist wants to say?

SPEAKING

6 SPEAKING Comparing photos

Look at picture 1 on the left and describe what it shows. What are the advantages and disadvantages of going on holiday with your family? Then look at picture 2 and describe it. What is good or bad about going on holiday with your friends? Which of the two do you think is better and why? Make two questions for each picture.

1

2

7 WRITING A questionnaire

Answer the questions. Write at least one to two sentences for each question.

QUESTIONNAIRE: FRIENDSHIP

1 How important are friends to you? ______

2 Is it better to have lots of friends or only one or two good friends? Why? ______

3 How often do you see your best friend(s)? ______

4 How much time do you spend with your friends every week? ______

5 How long have you known your best friend? ______

6 What hobbies or interests do you share with your friends? ______

7 What should a good friend be like? ______

8 Nobody is perfect. Why would you end a friendship? Give an example. ______

8 WRITING A picture story

Tell the picture story. Write at least two sentences for each picture. You can use the words given or your own ideas.

Anna – boyfriend – dump – new girlfriend?

phone best friend – cry – advice – shouldn't sit at home

decide – visit cousin – weekend – go on moped

leave home – on moped – rain

an hour later – stop – café – nice young guy – see Anna

sit – next table – chat – half an hour – laugh – like each other

leave café together – will meet the next day – forget old boyfriend

9 WRITING What's your opinion?

Choose one statement and write your opinion about it. Give reasons and examples and sum up your opinion. Write about 100 words.

1. You can learn a lot about friends and relationships from soap operas.
2. Being a teenager has its good and bad points.
3. Teenagers spend too much time on computer and video games.

10 WRITING A report

Choose one of the following topics and write a report of about 100 words.

1. Our last family holiday
2. My favourite film
3. A good day in town with my friends

11 MEDIATION A letter to a problem page

a) You read about a problem in a UK teen magazine. You also read the advice.

I can't forget him

I went out with a really nice boy for four months. We had the same interests and it was always fun with him. I thought I had found the boy of my dreams, but then he said he just wanted to be friends. He dumped me without a reason. That was four weeks ago. He doesn't answer my calls or e-mails. I expect he's going out with someone new and doesn't want to tell me. I'm really unhappy because I miss him and I can't forget him. What should I do?

Charlotte, 16

Dear Charlotte,

There's only one good way to forget an unhappy relationship – find a new exciting one! But first, do things that help to get HIM out of your life. Throw away photos and letters, delete[1] videos, phone numbers, e-mails and e-mail address. Throw away everything that reminds[2] you of the time you were together. Don't play romantic music or watch romantic films. Don't listen to song texts about unhappy love – and don't watch happy couples on the street! When you find yourself thinking about him, call a friend, go shopping and buy yourself something new, help in the kitchen, read a book or do homework – anything to make you think of other things. Don't go to bed until you are really tired, or you may lie awake[3] for hours.

Now that you have more time alone, do the things that you never had time for when you were together. Do sports, join a club, go to the cinema with your girl friends. Don't go to places that you went to with HIM. Go to new places and meet new people!

Remember, this happens to everyone at some time, so talk to your friends and let them help you too.

Your mag team

b) You have a German friend who is in the same situation as Charlotte. In a short e-mail to your friend, write notes in German about the advice in the UK magazine.

12 MEDIATION A film

Read about the German film Crazy. Explain to an English friend in English what the film is about. Write notes.

Crazy

Benni ist 16 und halbseitig gelähmt. Aufgrund seiner schlechten Schulnoten in Mathematik wird er von seinen Eltern in ein Internat geschickt. Er hat ein paar Mal die Schule gewechselt. Meist war es für Benni schwer, Freunde zu finden. Diesmal geht es einfacher – zunächst. Er teilt ein Zimmer mit Janosch. Dieser ist jedoch mehr an Spaß und Mädchen als an der Schule interessiert. Die Jungen freunden sich jedoch an – bis sich beide in ihre Klassenkameradin, die schöne Malen, verlieben. Dass das zu Konflikten führt, ist klar. Die Freundschaft zwischen Benni und Janosch wird auf eine echte Probe gestellt. Ein Film über die schwierige Zeit des Erwachsenwerdens und das Spannungsfeld zwischen Freundschaft und Liebe. Aber auch Spaß und Abenteuer kommen nicht zu kurz.

[1]delete [dɪˈliːt] *löschen* [2]remind (sb. of sth.) [rɪˈmaɪnd] *(jdn. an etw.) erinnern* [3]lie awake [ˌlaɪ əˈweɪk] *wach liegen*

13 READING Daniel's blog

a) First read the whole text. Then complete the tasks.

Hi, friends!

Well, here I am in Oxford! My old friend Max and I are at a tennis camp – and it's brilliant! Two weeks of tennis, English language and culture, sightseeing and fun! My English is better already – as proof I'm writing my blog in English! Here's my news for the last few days.

Sunday, 1st August
We arrived at Heathrow from Cologne and were taken to Oxford in a minibus – with four annoying 10-year-olds (on the kids' course). After a good hour we arrived in Oxford – were happy to say goodbye to the screaming kids! Our accommodation[1] is great, nice student rooms in the Queen's College. We could have stayed with a host family[2] or at a youth hostel, but we thought college would be more fun. It is fun – but we have to be in bed at 10.30 – very uncool! On Sunday evening there was a barbecue, so we met the other students. Some are from the UK, but mainly from EU countries and Japan. International atmosphere. Cool! Max has fallen in love with a Spanish girl called Maria!

Monday, 2nd August
Had a great English breakfast (sausages, beans, eggs, bacon). First, the coaches watched us play and they put us into groups. Maria was put in the same group as me – sorry, Max, not my fault. There's also Sven from Sweden, Jean-Paul from somewhere near Paris, Anna from Poland, and a Greek girl called Elena. We have to speak English together. In my group we're all 16 to 18. English conversation in the afternoon with our teacher, Nina, was cool too. Just eight in our group, laughed a lot. Max didn't say much – couldn't take his eyes off Maria, but she doesn't seem to be interested (poor Max!).

Tuesday, 3rd August
Today I was bored with the discussion on tactics, strategy and mental attitude – I just want to play for fun, nothing too serious. But after lunch we did a city tour by open-top bus. Great! We saw all the city highlights[3], like some of the world's oldest colleges. One of them, Christ Church, is very special. Oh, – and parts of the Harry Potter books were filmed there, in the Great Hall (which is the Dining Hall at Hogwarts). After the tour we went into town with the guys in my group and Anna. We saw Maria and Elena in a shoe shop, so suddenly Max thought he needed new trainers … ! In the evening we all watched a DVD and chatted.

Thursday, 5th August
More sausages for breakfast, more tennis with Maria, more English conversation. In the evening we played volleyball or football. Some of us seem to be better at football than at tennis – including me!

Saturday 7th August
In the morning we had a boring video analysis of each player in our tennis groups – not cool when you try to do a perfect stroke[4] but miss the ball! Tomorrow we're all going on a trip to London. Brilliant! I'll tell you about it in my next blog.
Daniel

b) Tick A, B or C.

1 The blog is …

- A from an English boy who is doing a tennis course in Oxford.
- B from a German boy who is doing an English course in Oxford.
- C from a German boy who is doing a tennis course with English classes in Oxford.

2 The journey from Heathrow to Oxford took …

A an hour. B less than an hour. C more than an hour.

[1]accommodation [əkɒmə'deɪʃn] *Unterkunft* [2]host family ['həʊst fæməli] *Gastfamilie* [3]highlight ['haɪlaɪt] *Höhepunkt* [4]stroke [strəʊk] *Schlag*

3 Daniel and Max are staying ...

- A at a youth hostel.
- B with an Oxford family.
- C in college rooms.

4 Daniel is ...

- A 16 years old.
- B between 16 and 18.
- C over 18.

5 In Daniel's tennis group there are ... students.

- A five
- B six
- C eight

Christ Church, Oxford

c) Tick the correct box.

	True	False	Not given
1 Daniel has known Max a long time.	☐	☐	☐
2 Max fancies Nina.	☐	☐	☐
3 Elena is from Athens.	☐	☐	☐
4 The name of the English teacher is Anna.	☐	☐	☐
5 Daniel doesn't take the tennis course too seriously.	☐	☐	☐
6 Scenes from the Harry Potter films were filmed at Christ Church.	☐	☐	☐
7 Max wanted to buy new trainers because Maria was also looking at shoes.	☐	☐	☐
8 One evening Daniel and Max went to the cinema.	☐	☐	☐
9 Tennis is the game that Daniel plays best.	☐	☐	☐
10 A visit to London is planned for Sunday.	☐	☐	☐

d) Answer the questions.

1 Which countries are they from?

Maria: ______ Nina: ______ Max: ______ Anna: ______

Sven: ______ Jean-Paul: ______ Elena: ______

2 What did Daniel like about his stay in Oxford? Write four things.

______

______

______

3 What didn't Daniel like very much? Write two things.

______

______

______

14 USE OF LANGUAGE A first date

a) Read the magazine article. Underline the correct form in the brackets.

Some things (have changed/changed) since your parents (gone/went) on their first date, but lots of things are still the same. We asked our readers what (advice/advise) they would give others of the same sex (which/who) are going on a first date. Here are some of the answers:

The girls said:

Make sure you're going to do something both of you enjoy (done/doing). For example, if your date wants to see a scary movie or he wants to go to a boxing match and you hate those things, tell him and do something else. Try to get to the meeting place (by/to) the time you agreed. Nobody likes (a stand/to stand) around in the cold. Dress (careful/carefully). Don't wear your oldest jeans with holes or shoes you can't walk in. Don't talk (about/over) your terrible ex-boyfriend. And don't agree (with/by) all your date's opinions. That's boring.

The boys said:

Don't be late! Be yourself, don't play a role. Don't be nervous, be natural and (relaxing/relaxed). Don't talk about (you/yourself) too much. Don't (talk/tell) stupid jokes. Show that you're a good listener. Don't talk about problems with your parents. Talk about fun things – music, concerts, movies. Don't tell your date about your fantastic friends – she may be more interested in them (than/as) in you! Don't worry that your date could be disappointed in you. If the evening doesn't go (good/well), better luck next time!

b) Match the words from the text with the correct definition. There is one definition that you don't need.

WORD	DEFINITION
1 scary	A what you feel or think about something or somebody
2 agree	B the way you feel when something is not as good as you hoped
3 opinion	C think the same as somebody
4 date	D something that makes you feel afraid
5 disappointed	E a romantic meeting
6 worry	F a funny story that makes you laugh
	G be afraid that something bad or unpleasant might happen

Word	1	2	3	4	5	6
Definition						

c) Find words in the text in a) that mean more or less the same.

1 put on: *wear* ______ 2 film: ______

3 point of view: ______ 4 part : ______

d) Find opposites in the text in a).

1 different: *same* ______ 2 hate: ______

3 exciting: ______ 4 early: ______

How did you do?

Schau dir die Lösungen der Aufgaben auf der S. 72 an. Beantworte dann die Fragen unten. Wenn du mit No antwortest oder einfach mehr üben möchtest, kannst du die angegebenen Aufgaben im Workbook (▸ pp. 44–65) lösen.

1–3 LISTENING Friends on the net, Voicemail messages, Talking about …	Yes	No	Exercise
1 Konntest du nach dem 1. Hören beurteilen, um was es im Wesentlichen geht?	☐	☐	▸ 1–2
2 Hast du die Detailfragen ohne Probleme beantworten können?	☐	☐	▸ 3–5, 9, 10
3 Hast du Zahlen, Daten, Uhrzeiten, Telefonnummern usw. richtig verstanden?	☐	☐	▸ 3, 4
4 Konntest du den amerikanischen und australischen Akzent erkennen und verstehen?	☐	☐	▸ 6, 7
5 Konntest du dem Sprechtempo gut folgen?	☐	☐	▸ 8
4–6 SPEAKING Dumped, A cartoon, Comparing photos			
1 Hast du mit dem *present progressive* (z. B. *he's reading*) beschrieben, was die Personen auf den Bildern gerade tun?	☐	☐	▸ 27
2 Hast du wichtige Vokabeln für die Bildbeschreibung (*in the foreground* usw.) gewusst?	☐	☐	▸ 11
3 Hast du die Personen und die Atmosphäre der Bilder mit passenden Adjektiven (*angry, happy, sad, hurt*) beschrieben?	☐	☐	▸ 11
4 Hast du problemlos Fragen stellen und Fragen beantworten können?	☐	☐	▸ 12, 28
5 Hast du die zwei Fotos problemlos vergleichen können?	☐	☐	▸ 13
6 Hast du den Cartoon und die Aussage des Cartoon-Zeichners beschreiben können?	☐	☐	▸ 14
7 WRITING A questionnaire			
1 Hast du passende Vokabeln für eine Personenbeschreibung (z. B. *reliable, honest*) gewusst?	☐	☐	▸ 30
2 Hast du passende Vokabeln für Freizeit und Hobbys (z. B. *hang out, surf the net*) gewusst?	☐	☐	▸ 18, 31
3 Hast du deine Rechtschreibung und Grammatik überprüft und deine Fehler korrigiert?	☐	☐	▸ 17
8 WRITING A picture story			
1 Hast du die *story* hauptsächlich im *simple past* und *past progressive* geschrieben?	☐	☐	▸ 29
2 Hast du passende Adjektive und Adverbien benutzt, um deine *story* auszuschmücken?	☐	☐	▸ 15
9 WRITING What's your opinion?			
1 Hast du deinen Text richtig strukturiert und mit Argumenten dafür oder dagegen belegt?	☐	☐	▸ 13, 18
2 Hast du passende Satzadverbien (z.B. *First, …/ Second, …/ Finally, …, For example …*) für die Reihenfolge deiner Argumente verwendet?	☐	☐	▸ 18
10 WRITING A report			
1 Hast du deine Ideen mithilfe eines *brainstorming* gesammelt?	☐	☐	▸ 18
2 Hast du die 5Ws (*who, what, when, where, why + how*) am Anfang deines Textes berücksichtigt?	☐	☐	▸ 19
3 Hast du für die Themen 1 und 3 das *simple past* (z.B. *we went*) und *past progressive* (z.B. *we were walking*) benutzt?	☐	☐	▸ 29
4 Hast du für die Beschreibung eines Films das *simple present* (z.B. *it is*) und *present progressive* (z.B. *is going*) benutzt?	☐	☐	▸ 27
5 Hast du *linking words* (z. B. *although, because, when, so, after*, etc.) verwendet?	☐	☐	▸ 16
11, 12 MEDIATION A letter to a problem page, A film			
1 Hast du darauf geachtet, mit eigenen Worten nur das Wesentliche weiterzugeben bzw. nicht alles wörtlich zu übersetzen?	☐	☐	▸ 23–26
2 Hast du für unbekannte Wörter Umschreibungen (*paraphrasing*) benutzt?	☐	☐	▸ 32
13 READING Daniel's blog			
1 Konntest du schnell herausfinden, um was es in dem Text geht?	☐	☐	▸ 20a, 22a
2 Hast du nach Schlüsselwörtern (*key words*) gesucht, um Antworten zu finden?	☐	☐	▸ 20b/c, 22b/c
3 Hast du die Bedeutung unbekannter Wörter erschließen können?	☐	☐	▸ 21
14 USE OF LANGUAGE A first date			
1 Hast du die richtigen Wörter aus *word families* finden können?	☐	☐	▸ 33
2 Hast du die korrekten Präpositionen (z.B. *in, at, to*) finden können?	☐	☐	▸ 34
3 Hast du Gegensätze (*opposites*) im Text erkennen können?	☐	☐	▸ 35

Unit 2 The world we live in

1 Modern appliances ▸ p. 28

a) Read p. 28 of your student's book again. Then label the pictures.

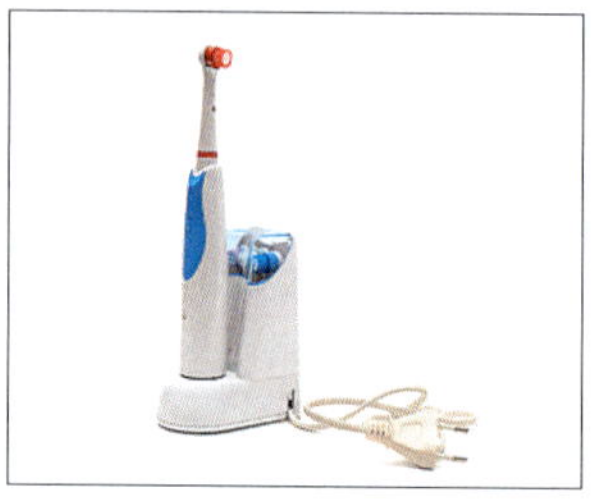

electric toothbrush

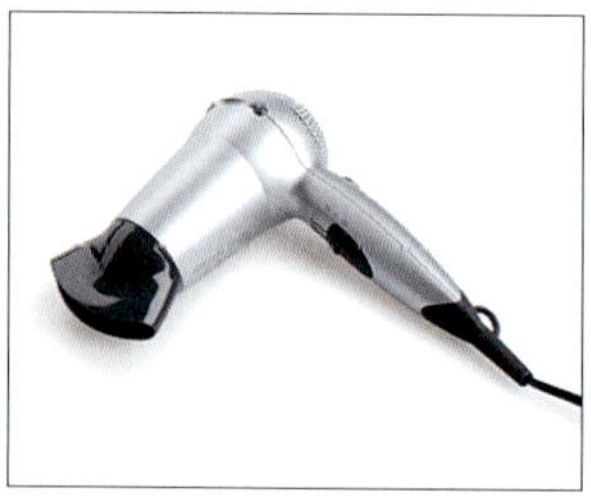

b) Modern appliances in my home. Write a list. Use a dictionary for words you don't know.

mobile phone, computer,

c) Choose four things from a) and b). Say what you or others in your family use them for. How often do you (or others) use these things? For how long do you (or others) use them? Write a few sentences about each thing.

Washing machine: I think my mother uses the washing machine once or twice a week. I expect she uses it for about an hour.

1

2

3

4

2201
2202

2 LISTENING My family and our toys[1]

▸ p. 28 • WB (p. 66) 6

Listen to what Mel says about her family's use of energy. Read the questions below first. Then answer them in a few words.

1 How many computers are there in Mel's family? ______

2 Who has got a games console, a mobile and an MP3 player? ______

3 Who has got an e-reader? ______

4 Who uses social networking sites regularly? ______

5 Which appliances do they use in the bathroom? ______

6 How many cars are there in the family? ______

7 Are the cars petrol-driven or diesel? ______

8 How do Mel and her brother get to school? ______

WB, pp. 44–48

9 Who goes by bike regularly? ______

2302

10 Does anyone in the family talk about saving energy? ______

3 REVISION Ask Mel (Simple present: wh-questions)

▸ p. 28 • GF 2 (p. 151) 6

Listen to what Mel says in exercise 2 again (6). You want to know more about her family's use of energy. Put the words in the correct order to make more questions with question words.

1 send/How many/every day/do/text messages/you?

How many text messages do you send every day?

2 use/appliances/do/Which/the kitchen/you/in?

______

3 your family/there/How many/in/mobiles/are?

______

4 by bus/you/train/do/or/go/How often?

2303

______

4 REVISION Our carbon footprint (Simple present: active and passive)

▸ p. 29 • GF 6 (p. 156)

Choose and underline the correct form.

A lot of energy (is needed/needs) for all the machines and appliances that we (are used/use) every day. When we (produce/are produced) energy, carbon dioxide (CO_2) (sends/is sent) into the air. CO_2 is a greenhouse gas which (causes/is caused) global warming. The number of tonnes of CO_2 that you (produce/are produced) in a year (call/is called) your carbon footprint. In Germany 11 tonnes of CO_2 (are produced/produce) by each person. Your carbon footprint (is got/gets) bigger every time you (are watched/watch) television or (are gone/go) by car. But remember, we can all help to reduce our carbon footprint by walking and cycling!

2304

[1]toy [tɔɪ] *Spielzeug*

5 REVISION Modern inventions (Passive: simple past)

▸ p. 30 • GF 6 (p. 156)

Underline the correct form.

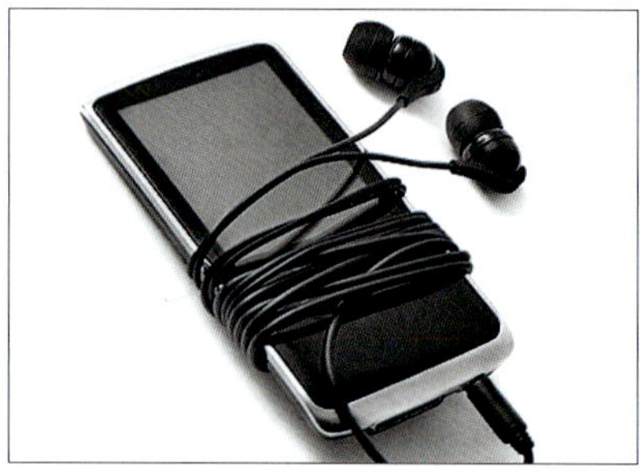

1 Facebook (was created/had created) in 2003.
2 TV dinners (first sold/were first sold) in the 1970s.
3 Trainers (had first worn/were first worn) only for sports.
4 Modern trainers (were worn/wore) for fashion in the 1970s.
5 GPS technology (were developed/was developed) for the US army.
2405 6 The iPod® (was invented/were invented) by Apple in 2000.

6 WORDS Word families (Nouns from verbs)

▸ p. 30, p. 167

Write a noun from each verb. Tip: One noun is the same as its verb.

Verb	Noun	Verb	Noun
1 act	– *action*	5 heat	– heating
2 invent	– invention	6 discuss	– discussion
3 choose	– ______	7 inform	– information
4 pollute	– pullutetion	8 present	– presentation

b) *Complete the sentences with words from a) in the correct form.*

1 The computer and the mobile phone were fantastic invention.
2 You use energy every time you chees water or watch television.
3 You can ______ the environment or help to save it.
It's your Choice.
2406 4 We should act quickly to save energy and reduce water and air pullution.

7 WORDS Odd word out

▸ p. 32

Which word does not fit in the group? Underline the odd word out.

1 global warming: greenhouse gases • climate change • pullover • carbon footprint
2 things in the kitchen: cooker • microwave • conditions • dishwasher • fridge
3 transport: car • lorry • train • bus • machine • tram
4 electronic appliances: computer • games console • greenhouse • mobile phone
5 things in the bathroom: toothbrush • target • electric razor • hairdryer
2407 6 inventions: social networking sites • GPS technology • TV dinners • scientist • iPod®

[1]trap [træp] *gefangen halten*

8 SPEAKING Compliments

▸ p. 33 • WB (pp. 67–68)

Imagine that you meet Jake Martin after the science competition. You are impressed by his gasifier. What would you say to him? Choose from the box.

> congratulations • Well done! • You've done a very good job. • What an interesting project! • I really like your idea.

You First of all, congratulations, Jake! – [Sag ihm, dass du gratulierst.]

I really like your idea – [Sag ihm, dass seine Idee dir wirklich gut gefällt.]

You have done a great job – [Sag ihm, er hat tolle Arbeit geleistet.]

Jake Oh, thank you. I'm glad to hear that.

You What a interesting project – [Sag ihm, was für ein interessantes Projekt es ist.]

Jake Well, that's a nice compliment.

You Well done! – [Sag ihm, dass er es gut gemacht hat]

WB, pp. 49–51

9 MEDIATION Flight check-in[1] service

▸ p. 33 • WB (pp. 69–70)

Test

Morgen fliegst du von London Gatwick mit einem Freund nach Deutschland zurück. Erkläre ihm auf Deutsch, wie man am bequemsten die Bordkarten bekommt, ohne am Flughafen in der Schlange stehen zu müssen.

> Save time with our **FlyEasy online check-in service!**
>
> You can check in as early as 22 hours before your flight departure[2]. Enter *flyeasy.com>online check-in* and give us your name and your booking code. You can print out your boarding pass[3] at home or at work. You can even choose your seat[4]. When you get to the airport, you simply check in your baggage[5] at one of our baggage counters[6] and go straight to your gate. There's no waiting! It's quick and easy.
>
> With our **mobile check-in service** you can check in from your smartphone. Just click *Check in*. Enter your name and booking code and choose your seat. Your mobile boarding pass will be sent directly to your phone. **We wish you a good flight!**

WB, pp. 60–61

10 WORDS Get it right! (Prepositions)

▸ p. 35

Complete the sentences with the correct prepositions: about, at, by, for, in, into, of, without.

1 Are you interested in reading about global warming?

2 One reason for climate change is that producing energy sends CO_2 into the air.

3 Not only industry and cars are responsible for CO_2 in the air.

4 Life ~~without~~ of modern appliances wouldn't be very easy.

5 Modern kitchens are full of useful electric appliances.

6 We can help to slow down global warming by walking and cycling more.

7 Everybody can do something to help. Are you good ~~in~~ at saving energy and reducing your carbon footprint?

2510

[1]check in [ˈtʃekɪn] *einchecken* [2]departure [dɪˈpɑːtʃə] *Start* [3]boarding pass [ˈbɔːdɪŋ pɑːs] *Bordkarte* [4]seat [siːt] *Sitz, Sitzplatz* [5]baggage [ˈbæɡɪdʒ] *Gepäck* [6]baggage counter [ˈbæɡɪdʒ ˈkaʊntə] *Gepäckabgabe*

11 READING WORKING WITH THE TEXT
The Carbon Diaries 2015

▸ pp. 34–35 • WB (pp. 66–67)

a) *Read pp. 34–35 in your student's book again and match the sentence halves.*

1 The UK government introduces carbon rationing	for one hour a day.
2 Children have to give up carbon points	without their carbon rationing card.
3 People can't use buses	to reduce Britain's carbon footprint.
4 Laura can only heat her room	to help with the family carbon allowance.
5 Laura and her mum had to get off the bus	makes Laura feel scared.
6 Students pay for college heating with their cards	because her mum couldn't find her carbon card.
7 Laura and her family	but it's very cold anyway.
8 The cold, dark house	don't spend time together any more.

b) *What is the Browns' life like under the carbon rationing system? Write at least five things from the text.*

The Browns' family life has changed completely.

The family is disappeard.
5 minutes shower and baths only on weekend.
It's all kind of a choice.
Her eys was filled with tears as we walked past the school

c) *Why does Mrs Brown tell Laura that she's sorry and that she feels responsible for her generation? (ll. 55–58). What have they messed up? What does she mean? Explain in a few sentences.*

Mrs Brown means that it's hers fault, because she thinks that her generation is responsible for this was happend. Because of that her daughter hasn't freetime and she can't be happy.

d) *Does the story scare you? Does it make you think? Write your opinion.*

The story scares me because the system controls everybody's life.

The story give me a sin to save more energy, because it's so difficult with this system, I woulden't be have freetime.

WB, pp. 56–59

Now you

How could you and your family save carbon points if you had to? Ideas: **saving electricity, water, petrol, heating.** *Write notes in your exercise book and discuss your answers in class.*

I could use my ... less and I would remember to ... I think my sister/brother could ...

12 WORDS Helping the environment

▸ p. 36

a) Match.

Take	less meat
Eat	more trees
Plant	shorter showers
Use	rubbish
Recycle	paper, plastic and glass
Reduce	low-energy appliances

b) Choose four things from a) above and write four sentences with **because**.

We should plant more trees because they reduce CO_2 in the air.

1 __________

2 __________

3 __________

2712 4 __________

13 WORDS Opposites

▸ p. 36

Find and write pairs of opposites.

agree • attractive • borrow • clean • cold • dangerous • dirty • *disagree* • heat • high • lend • low • safe • strong • unattractive • weak

agree – disagree

2713

14 SPEAKING Talking about cartoons

▸ p. 36 • WB (pp. 67–68)

Test

Describe the cartoon. Make notes in your exercise book and discuss your answers in class.

1 What can you see in the picture (people and place)?
A boy is in the library. There's a woman ....

2 What is happening? Who is saying what?
The boy has read the sign. He is asking ...

3 What is the message? What does the cartoon artist want to tell the reader?
I think the cartoon artist wants to tell/show the reader that ...

4 Do you think the cartoon is easy to understand?
Do you agree with the cartoon's message?

VB, pp. 9–51

"Excuse me, but do you have any books?"

15 Quiz: How green are you? ▸ p. 36

Read the questions and tick a box. Be honest!

1 How often do you buy pizza or fast food?

A Often. B Sometimes. C Not very often.

2 How do you buy cola or other soft drinks? In ...

A plastic bottles. B cans[1]. C glass bottles.

3 The television is on, but nobody is watching it. Do you ...?

A leave it on B turn it off
C leave it to others to decide

4 You're the last person to leave a room. Do you turn the lights off?

A Always. B Sometimes. C Never.

5 When you go shopping in a supermarket, do you ..?

A buy a plastic bag B use an old plastic bag C take a basket or a cloth[2] bag with you

6 What do you do with old comics and magazines?

A Throw them away with the rubbish. B Put them in a bin for recycling.
C Give them to your friends so it's their problem.

7 When you clean your teeth, do you ...?

A turn the water on and off as you need it B leave the water running all the time
C use just one glass of water

8 When the place where you're going isn't far, do you ...?

A walk or cycle B ask a parent to drive you C take a bus

9 Do you make a lot of calls on your mobile?

A Yes, often. B No, I try not to. C Yes, sometimes.

10 On average, how many text messages do you send every day?

A Under five. B Five to ten. C More than ten.

Count your points.

1	A 0	B 1	C 2
2	A 0	B 0	C 2
3	A 0	B 2	C 1
4	A 2	B 1	C 0
5	A 0	B 1	C 2
6	A 0	B 2	C 0
7	A 1	B 0	C 2
8	A 2	B 0	C 1
9	A 0	B 2	C 1
10	A 2	B 1	C 0

20–15 points:	Well done! You think about the environment. You try hard to save energy and water.
10–14 points:	You are doing OK, but you should try still harder.
Under 10 points:	Well, you still have a long way to go! Maybe you should think more seriously about your carbon footprint. Helping to save energy and water is not just for others.

[1]can [kæn] *Dose* [2]cloth [klɒθ] *Stoff*

16 WORDS 'Green' or 'non-green'?

▸ p. 37

a) Write the words and phrases in two lists: 'green' and 'non-green'.

carbon dioxide • climate change • destroy[1] forests • global warming • greenhouse gases • *insulation*[2] • low-energy products • plant trees • plastic bags • pollution • recycle • reduce our carbon footprint • solar power

☺ *insulation,* ______________________________

____

☹ *carbon dioxide,* ______________________________

____

b) What do these teenagers say about global warming? Fill in words and phrases from a) above.

We always buy ______________ products, like low-energy fridges, so we save energy and money.

In our family we ______________ all our old newspapers, glass and plastic too.

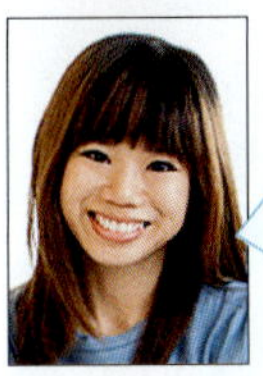

If people don't do more to stop ______________, ice at the poles will start to melt.

We try to ______________ ______________ by walking and cycling, so we use less petrol now.

I eat less meat now, because in some countries they ______________ to make room[3] for cattle stations[4].

Our house has good ______________ so we can keep all the rooms warm and reduce heating costs.

We should use more ______________ It could be produced more cheaply in hot countries.

I never buy ______________ in supermarkets. I always take my cloth bag or a basket with me.

2916

17 WRITING Making schools greener (A written discussion)

▸ p. 37 • SF (p. 146)

Produce a written discussion for and against this statement: **We can do more to make schools greener.**

Ideas: ***use recycled paper, don't make so many photocopies, don't use throwaway plastic pens, turn off heating, lights, computers, electronic equipment when not needed***

1 Introduction (Say what you are writing about and why the topic is important.)
This topic is important because schools could also help to slow down global warming. If we don't …

2 Arguments (Write arguments for and against the statement.)
2.1 First argument (with example or reason. Start a new paragraph for each idea.)
2.2 Second argument (with example or reason. Start a new paragraph for each idea.)
2.3 …
A lot of people think that … First, … Second, … Another argument/reason/example is that … Finally, …

WB, pp. 52–55

3 Conclusion (sum up the arguments and give your own opinion)
To sum up, I think … That's why … In my opinion, it is clear that … There are more arguments for the statement than against it …

2918
2919

[1]destroy [dɪ'strɔɪ] *zerstören* [2]insulation [ˌɪnsju'leɪʃn] *Isolierung* [3]make room *Platz schaffen* [4]cattle station ['kætl ˌsteɪʃn] *Viehfarm*

Unit 3 Have your say!

1 Teen issues ▸ pp. 46–47

a) Youth magazine Teen Voice asked 14- to 17-year-olds what kind of things they cared about. Read some of the answers:

Mara

I care about our pets, so I work in a rescue centre for lost and unwanted pets at the weekends. I feed them, clean their cages and take the dogs for walks. They are so excited when we play with them.

I like doing volunteer work. I'm in a church group that looks after old people who live alone. We visit them, do shopping for them, just talk to them. They're happy when we spend time with them.

Kate

I think that teenage troublemakers are becoming a real problem. Sometimes kids carry knives, even guns. You never really feel safe in some parts of town, not even in the daytime.

Ben

Ed

I'm in a group that does clean-up projects. I hate it when people throw rubbish in fields, like car tyres[2] and even old sofas. You can't imagine what we find!

Beth

I think we need to know what's happening in our country, for example with new laws about education and jobs, because that's important for our future. I watch the news on TV sometimes.

We have some kids in our class from Eastern Europe. My classmates don't talk to them because they say they take away our jobs. But that isn't fair, and even if it was true, it isn't the kids' fault. I call it discrimination, and I find it stupid.

Josh

b) Who cares about what? Match what the teenagers said with the statements below. Then write the names. There are two statements that do not match.

1 _Kate_ likes to do social work in the community.

2 ________ is interested in the country's politics.

3 ________ helps at a home for animals.

4 ________ is worried about climate change.

5 ________ likes working for the environment.

6 ________ cares about people losing their jobs.

7 ________ cares about discrimination of immigrants.

8 ________ is worried about teenage crime.

c) Which of the issues in a) and b) do you think are the most important? Name two and say why you think so. Which of the issues could you perhaps get interested in or involved with? Write a paragraph in your exercise book.

3001 ***I think … is a very important issue for kids of my age because … What … said is true for me too. I think the same as … I think I could get involved in …***

2 WORDS What you can do ▸ p. 49

Choose and underline the correct word from the brackets.

Not only adults, but also young people have (rights/laws). If something is happening that you don't agree with, you can (have your way/have your say) and try to change it. But do you (save/care) enough? There are many (petitions/issues) which are important for young people. Some problems are close to home, in your town or (government/community). Maybe you think that young people need more (facilities/citizens) for sports and free time. If lots of young people think the same, you can start a (petition /percentage) and ask people to (sign/write) it. You can e-mail the local newspaper or radio station, go to the (town hall/government) to talk to the (citizens/town councillors). Somebody will listen. Other issues are important for your country, like education and jobs, (democracy/discrimination) against minorities, making the (equipment/environment) clean and healthy.

Many issues are important for people of all countries, like climate change and keeping (war/peace).

3102 Young people can't solve the world's problems alone, but they can show that they care by (speaking out/listening).

Now you ▸ SF (pp. 125–126)

a) *Describe the pictures. Say what you think the situation is. Remember to use the* ***present progressive*** *(e.g.* ***is sitting****) for things that are happening at the moment.*

1

2

Picture 1 shows ... In the foreground ... On the right/left ...

b) *What could young people in your school, community or town do to improve the situations in the pictures? What action could you take? Make notes in your exercise book and discuss your ideas in class.*

petition, campaign, e-mails to MP/town councillors ...

3 REVISION Rights

▸ p. 49

Fill in the correct preposition.

about • at (2x) • for (2x) • in • out of • to (2x) • under • without

1 Oliver's article is *about* young people's rights.

2 He says British teenagers ________ 18 have the right to be listened to.

3 They have the right to meet ________ public too.

4 But often teens can only go into shops two ________ a time and ________ bags.

5 When 16-year-olds go ________ the cinema, they pay adult prices.

6 ________ work 16-year-olds earn less than adults.

7 On the other hand, 16-year-olds can fight ________ their country.

8 They can apply ________ a job too.

9 But if they're under 18, they don't have the right ________ vote.

3203 10 In Britain, four ________ ________ five 16-year-olds find these things unfair.

4 LISTENING A teen discussion

▸ p. 50 • WB (p. 66) 7

Test

a) *You are going to hear four UK students talking about voting. First read the statements in tasks a) and b). Then listen and tick the correct boxes.*

1 The students talk about ...
- election promises. ☐
- the history of voting rights. ☐
- why it is important to use your right to vote. ☐

2 Which students think voting is very important?
- The two girls. ☐
- One boy and one girl. ☐
- Just one girl. ☐

b) *Write **T** (true) or **F** (false) after each statement. Then listen again to check your answers.*

1 Fran's sister is going to vote at the next election. .... *F*

2 Tom thinks that politicians make promises but they don't keep them. .... ☐

3 Tom believes that every vote is important. .... ☐

4 Syed thinks it is stupid to complain about how the country is run if you don't vote. .... ☐

5 Syed thinks that the voting age should be 16. .... ☐

WB, pp. 44–48

6 Tom thinks everyone should get involved with politics and voting. .... ☐

7 The voting age in Austria is 16. .... ☐

3204 8 About 16% of young people in the UK have a job before they are 16. .... ☐

5 WORKING WITH THE TEXT A class debate

▸ p. 52–53 • WB (pp. 66–67)

a) Read pp. 52–53 of your student's book again. Then put the sentences in the correct order. Write the numbers 2–9 in the boxes.

1 Mr Neck tells the class that his son can't get a job as a firefighter. .... ☐
2 David Petrakis stands up to protest against Mr Neck's lesson. .... ☐
3 Mr Neck says the USA should have closed its borders to immigrants in 1900. .... ☐
4 In the History lesson Mr Neck writes the word 'immigration' on the board. 1
5 Mr Neck tells the class about his family history as American citizens. .... ☐
6 Lots of students put up their hands because they don't agree with Mr Neck. .... ☐
7 Mr Neck tells David to sit down and be quiet. .... ☐
8 David leaves the classroom in protest. .... ☐
9 Mr Neck closes the debate when one boy says something he doesn't want to hear. .... ☐

b) What are these words in German? Try to work out their meaning from the text. If that doesn't work, use a dictionary.

figure out (ll. 25, 30) ______________ xenophobic (l. 78) ______________

supporters (l. 54) ______________ principal (l. 82) ______________

smart (l. 64) ______________

● *c) Read what David says about Mr Neck's lesson (ll. 67–68, ll. 70–71, ll. 73–78). Explain David's opinion. Here are some ideas.*

David thinks …
Each student should … ***Mr Neck can't just …***
All American citizens … ***Mr Neck's lesson is …***

____
____
____
____
____
____
____
____
____
____
____

6 WORDS Word families ▸ p. 54

a) Complete the table with verbs, nouns or adjectives.

VERB		NOUN	NOUN		ADJECTIVE
assess	–	*assessment*	________	–	different
________	–	debate	________	–	interested
decide	–	________	politician	–	________
________	–	discrimination	________	–	poor
________	–	election	________	–	realistic
speak	–	________	________	–	strong

b) Complete the sentences with words from a) in the correct form.

1 Would you like to vote in your country's next *election* ?

2 Do you think 16-year-olds are ________ in politics?

3 It is against the law to ________ people because of their race, religion, age or sex.

4 Mr Neck wanted to have a ________ on immigration.

5 In the novel *Speak* David Petrakis holds a short ________ about the rights of all US citizens.

6 Mr Neck and David have strong ________ of opinion on the subject of immigration.

7 What did David ________ to do in protest against Mr Neck's History lesson?

8 David showed ________ of character.

3406 9 What is your ________ of Mr Neck's History lesson?

7 WORDS Choose the correct word ▸ p. 54

Underline the correct word from the brackets.

1 Young people often (care about/agree about/speak up) child poverty.

2 You can show that you want changes by (voting/signing/writing) a petition.

3 The 'mosquito' is a (machine/device/equipment) that most adults can't hear.

4 In the History class the (decision/debate/announcement) on immigration was very short.

5 David Petrakis said that free speech was a human (question/issue/right).

3407 6 David won Melinda's (respect/attitude/opinion) with his protest against Mr Neck's lesson.

8 READING Iqbal Masih ▸ p. 54 • WB (pp. 66–67)

Test

a) *Read the story of Iqbal.*

The story of Iqbal Masih

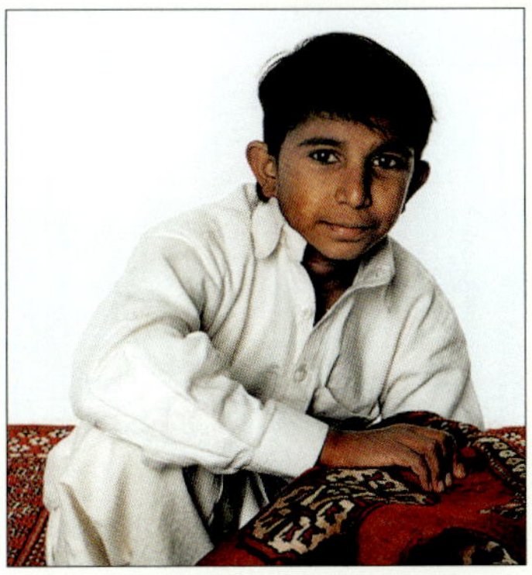

Iqbal Masih was born in a village in Pakistan in 1982. His parents did not have enough money to support the family, so when Iqbal was four, they sold him to a rich carpet[1]- maker for six years – for $200. The small child had to work 14 hours a day making carpets, in terrible conditions with little food. He worked together with many other children.

At the age of ten he was freed[2] by an organization in Pakistan which works against child labour[3]. Iqbal went to one of the organization's schools, with other children who had been child slaves. He was very intelligent, so he learned well. He was brave too and wanted to help to free other child workers. He stood up for the millions of child workers in Pakistan. In Europe and America he spoke out against the carpet trade. He told the world about the terrible conditions for child workers. He also asked people to boycott carpets from Pakistani companies that used child labour. He was successful, the world listened. People stopped buying carpets made in Pakistan. Sales fell heavily for three years, and Iqbal made many enemies in the carpet industry.

In 1994 Iqbal won the *Reebok Youth in Action Award* and he became known internationally as a child rights activist. Iqbal wanted to study in the USA and become a lawyer[4]. Brandeis University near Boston promised him a place after he had finished his school in Pakistan. But Iqbal had no future. In April 1995, at the age of thirteen, he was shot dead in his village in Pakistan. His death was officially reported as an accident. There are different reports about why he was killed and who killed him.

UNICEF believes that about 90% of the Pakistani carpet industry uses child workers. Now it is against the law to sell and buy children for child labour, but it still continues – and the law-breakers go free.

b) *Tick the correct box.*

The story is about …

Pakistani trade. ☐ family life in Pakistan. ☐ a child hero. ☐

c) *Match the sentence halves.*

Iqbal's parents sold him	when he was ten.
Iqbal worked	learned quickly and well.
He was freed	because they were too poor to feed him.
In school he	for a carpet company.
He wanted to	he became an activist for children's rights.
He was very brave and	study in the USA.
He was killed	when he was was thirteen.

WB, pp. 56–59

d) *In the text, mark the most important events in Iqbal's short life.*

e) *Imagine that it is now 2015. Iqbal hasn't been shot. He is still alive and he is now 33 years old. What is he doing today? Is he happy and successful? Write a short paragraph in your exercise book.*

3508

[1]carpet ['kɑːpɪt] *Teppich* [2]free *befreien* [3]child labour ['tʃaɪld ˌleɪbə] *Kinderarbeit* [4]lawyer ['lɔːjə] *Rechtsanwalt/-anwältin*

9 WORDS Opposites ▸ p. 54

a) Find and write pairs of opposites.

against • agree • attractive • borrow • cold • disagree • for • full-time • heat • high • lend • low • part-time • peace • save • thick • thin • unattractive • war • waste

against – for	________
________	________
________	________
________	________
________	________

b) Complete the sentences with word pairs from a).

1 Can you ________ me some money? – No, I can't. But maybe you can ________ some from Katie.

2 In the daytime desert temperatures are ________. But in the night they are ________.

3 We must ________ energy, not ________ it.

4 For most countries global warming will mean more ________ and less ________.

3609 5 Most governments of the world want ________, not ________.

10 WORDS Describing people and things ▸ p. 54

Match the words to the definitions.

A foreigner	is money that you have to pay to the government.
Trade	is a building where the local government works.
A tax	is someone who lives in or comes from a different country.
A town hall	is the act of buying and selling between two or more people or countries.

3610

11 WRITING Driving licence[1] at 17? ▸ p. 54 • WB (pp. 68–69)

In Germany, you have to be 18 years old to get a driving licence which allows you to drive alone. In the US you can get it at 16 and in the UK at 17. Should German teenagers be allowed to get a driving licence at 17 too? What do you think? Write five to six sentences in your exercise book. Give reasons for your opinion.

Allowing teenagers to get their driving licence at 17 sounds like a great/bad idea.
In my opinion, ...
I also think that ...
Maybe some young people ...
To sum it up I think ...

WB, pp. 52–55

[1]driving licence ['draɪvɪŋ 'laɪsns] *Führerschein*

12 MEDIATION Rules for alcohol in the UK

p. 54 • WB (pp. 69–70)

Test

a) If you are in the UK it is important to know what you can and can't do. For example, when and where you are allowed to drink alcohol. You have found some information on the internet. Take notes in German so that you can tell your friends. Don't translate. Write in your exercise book.

Teens and alcohol in the UK

Under 16
You are not allowed to buy or drink alcohol.
You are not allowed to enter a pub, a bar or a place where alcohol is sold or drunk without an adult.

16 and 17
If you are 16 or 17 you are allowed to drink wine or beer in a pub or restaurant, but only with a meal and only if an adult is with you. In Scotland, if you are 16 or 17 you can order wine or beer in a pub with a meal, but you needn't be with an adult.
You are not allowed to buy alcohol in shops or supermarkets.

18
You have to be 18 to buy and drink wine, beer and spirits[3] in a bar or a pub and to buy spirits in a shop or supermarket. Mostly you will be asked to show your ID[4]. It's illegal to buy alcohol for others who are under 18.

The rules for the minimum drinking age in the UK are not as strict as the rules in the USA.

b) Read page 54 of your student's book again about the rules for alcohol in the USA. Compare them with the rules in the UK. Write three sentences with comparisons.

WB, pp. 60–61

To buy and drink alcohol you have to be older in the USA than in the UK.

13 EVERYDAY ENGLISH SPEAKING Solving conflicts

p. 55 • WB (pp. 67–68)

Tick the best phrase in the situation: A, B or C.

1 (On a bus): You're staring at me. Is there a reason?
- A Oh, sorry. I didn't mean to stare. I was thinking about something else.
- B No. I wasn't staring. Why should I?
- C Mind your own business.

2 (In a restaurant): Hey, you! That's my jacket!
- A You're right. Mine is cleaner.
- B No, it isn't.
- C Sorry, I didn't mean to take it. Mine is under it.

3 (In a café): Excuse me. That's my seat[1].
- A Well, now it is mine.
- B I'm sorry. I didn't know it was taken.
- C So why aren't you sitting on it?

4 You're in a crowded café. Someone took your mobile by mistake and apologizes[2]. What do you say?
- A Idiot.
- B Be more careful next time.
- C OK. No worries.

5 On a bus, you're chatting and laughing loudly with a friend. Someone asks you to talk more quietly. What do you say?
- A Where's the problem?
- B We didn't mean to annoy you. Sorry.
- C Mind your own business.

6 A man asks you to take your bag off a bus seat, so he can sit down. What do you say?
- A Don't worry about it.
- B Can't you sit somewhere else?
- C Yes, of course. Sorry. I didn't see you.

WB, pp. 49–51

3713
3714
3715

[1]seat ['siːt] *Sitz, Sitzplatz* [2]apologize [ə'pɒlədʒaɪz] *sich entschuldigen* [3]spirits ['spɪrɪts] *Spirituosen* [4]ID = identification *Ausweis*

English for jobs

1 Preparing for an interview

▸ p. 67 • WB (pp. 67–68)

a) *Anton Schneider has applied to do an apprenticeship with Amcom, a US computer company in Berlin. To prepare for his interview in English he is making notes. Not all his ideas are good. Tick (✔) the statements and questions which are suitable, and cross (✘) the ones which are not.*

1 Would I have my own computer and telephone? ✘
2 My everyday English is quite good, and I'd like to improve it. ✔
3 Would I have to make coffee for everybody? ☐
4 Who would be my boss? ☐
5 Is the pay good? ☐
6 What would my working hours bc? ☐
7 I'm brilliant as a team leader. ☐
8 I like meeting new people and I love travelling. ☐
9 I already know a lot about the company from your website. ☐
10 I couldn't work late because I go to sport three times a week. ☐
11 I did work experience in an office last summer, and I didn't like it at all. The boss was terrible. ☐
12 I'm really interested in computers and I'd be very excited about working here. ☐
13 I hope I wouldn't have to start before 8.30. ☐
14 These offices are much nicer than the last place I worked in. ☐
15 I could work evenings or Saturdays if I had to. ☐
16 How long are the coffee breaks and how many do we get? ☐
17 I'd be brilliant with US visitors. I have American friends on Facebook. ☐
18 When will I hear from you? ☐

b) *How would you answer the following interview questions? Write a short paragraph for each answer.*

1 Can you tell me more about why you'd like to work for us?
Ideas: ***learn a lot, read about products, like speaking English***

I'm very interested in computers and I know quite a lot about them.

2 Tell me something about your strengths. What are you good at?
Ideas: ***very interested in ..., reliable, helpful, friendly, hard-working, good at organizing, like working in a team.***

I did work experience last summer and my boss said I

3801

2 Phoning about an appointment ▸ p. 68 • WB (pp. 67–68) 8

a) Lena would like to do an apprenticeship at a UK fashion company in Hamburg. She has received an invitation to an interview with Mr Jerome Hill. She calls the company to accept the invitation. What should Lena say? Tick A or B.

Sandra — *Fashions 21*, Sandra Moss speaking. How can I help you, please?

Lena — A Good morning. I'm calling about an interview with Mr Hill.

B I want to speak to Jerome Hill, please.

Sandra — I see. May I ask who's calling, please?

Lena — A Lena Hartmann.

B Yes, this is Lena Hartmann.

Sandra — Just a moment please, Ms Hartmann. I'll put you through to Mr Hill's assistant.

Lena — A Thank you.

B OK.

Sandra — I'm sorry to keep you waiting, but nobody's answering. Would you like to hold?

Lena — A No.

B Erm ..., no, thank you. It's OK. I'll try again later.

Sandra — Would you like to leave a message?

Lena — A Well, yes, if I may. Would you please tell Mr Hill or his assistant that I'll be happy to come for an interview on Friday at ten thirty?

B Yeah. Why not? Tell Mr Hill I'll be there on Friday at ten thirty. OK?

Sandra — So that's Ms Hartmann for an interview with Mr Hill on Friday at ten thirty. I'll tell Mr Hill as soon as possible.

Lena — A Thank you. Goodbye.

B OK. See you.

Sanda — You're welcome. Goodbye.

b) Listen (8) and check your answers.

c) Use phrases from a) above to write the following sentences in English.

1 Wer spricht, bitte? ______

2 Moment, bitte. Ich verbinde. ______

3 Niemand geht ran. ______

4 Bleiben Sie bitte am Apparat. ______

5 Ich versuche es später noch mal. ______

6 Kann ich etwas ausrichten? ______

7 Würden Sie bitte Mr Hill ausrichten, dass ... ______

3902 8 Gern geschehen. ______

[1]accept [ək'sept] *annehmen*

3 Arriving for an interview ▸ p. 69 • WB (pp. 67–68) 🎧 9

a) Lena has arrived for her interview and is talking to the receptionist[1]. Write the dialogue in the correct order in your exercise book. (R= receptionist, L = Lena)

R	Right, Ms Hartmann. I'll let Mr Hill know that you've arrived. Erm, ... would you like to sign the visitors' book, please?	
R	Just here on the right, please.	
R	Good morning. Can I help you?	1
L	Oh, good. Thank you.	
R	Could I have your name, please?	
L	Yes, of course. Where do I sign?	
L	Good morning. I have an interview with Mr Hill at ten thirty.	2
R	I'm afraid Mr Hill isn't answering, but I'll call his assistant.	
L	Yes, it's Hartmann, Lena Hartmann.	
R	You're welcome.	
R	OK. Mr Hill is expecting you now. His assistant will be here in a moment to pick you up.	

b) Listen to your CD (🎧 9) and check that you have the correct order.

c) Find at least two phrases in the dialogue that are typical of polite English. Write them down with their German translations.

4003

4 Polite small talk ▸ p. 69 • WB (pp. 67–68)

Jane, Mr Hill's assistant, meets Lena at reception. On the way up in the lift, Jane makes friendly conversation with Lena. Use the notes to write a short dialogue in English in your exercise book.

- Jane introduces herself to Lena.
- Lena tells Jane who she is.
- Jane asks Lena to follow her to the lifts. She tells her that they are going up to the fourth floor.
- Jane asks Lena if she found the way easily.
- Lena answers that it was no problem. The bus ride took only half an hour.
- Lena asks Jane if there are other candidates for interview.
- Jane tells Lena that she is the only one today.
- On the fourth floor Jane shows Lena where Mr Hill's office is and asks her to wait outside.
- Jane says that Mr Hill will see her in a few minutes.
- Lena thanks Jane.

Jane Hello, my name's Jane Kelly. I'm Mr Hill's assistant.
Lena Oh, hello. My name's Lena Hartmann.
Jane Would you like to...
On the fourth floor:
4004 *Jane Mr Hill's office...*

[1]receptionist [rɪˈsepʃənɪst] *Rezeptionist/-in, Empfangsdame*

5 An interview

▸ p. 69 • WB (pp. 67–68) 🎧 10, 11

a) *Mr Hill asks Lena into his office. Take Lena's role and answer Mr Hill's questions. Make notes first, then listen (🎧 10) and speak in the pauses. Use polite phrases and small talk. Don't answer with only yes or no.*

Mr Hill Hello, Lena. My name's Jerome Hill. Do sit down.

Lena Nice to meet you, Mr Hill. Thank you.

Mr Hill Did you find us easily?

Lena ______________________________

Mr Hill Would you like some tea or coffee? Or water perhaps?

Lena (says no politely) ______________________________

Mr Hill Well, thank you for your interest in our company. Perhaps you could tell me why you'd like to do your apprenticeship with us.

Lena ______________________________

____

Mr Hill I see. Perhaps you could tell me a little about your strengths. Why should we choose you?

Lena ______________________________

____

____

____

____

Mr Hill Good. Now what about school, Lena. How are your grades?

Lena ______________________________

Mr Hill That's what you'd need most here. We have lots of visitors from the UK. Sometimes from the USA too. Do you think you would be good at looking after visitors?

Lena ______________________________

Mr Hill OK. Now tell me, Lena. When could you start if we offered you an apprenticeship?

Lena ______________________________

Mr Hill Well, Lena, I think that's all for today. Thank you for coming. You'll hear from us early next week. Oh, and about the reference. Could you send it to us as soon as possible?

b) *Now listen to the complete interview (🎧 11). Check that your answers were similar to Lena's.*

c) *Write two good general questions to ask at an interview. The questions should show your interest.*

1 ______________________________

4105 2 ______________________________

6 A thank-you letter ▸ p. 69 • SF (p. 145)

a) After the interview Lena writes a short thank-you letter to the interviewer. Lena's English teacher gives her this advice:

- Thank Mr Hill for inviting you to the interview yesterday.
- Say that you enjoyed meeting him.
- Say you were impressed by the friendly atmosphere in the company.
- Say that you are very interested in working for *Fashion 21.*
- Say you would be able to start from 1st July.
- Give the name and telephone number of the person who will give you a reference.
- Say that you look forward to hearing from him.

Write the main part and the end of Lena's letter. If you write the letter on your computer, see p. 145 of your student's book for help with formal letters.

...
Dear Mr Hill

I am writing to ______________________________

____

____

____

____

____

____

Mr K. Johannsen will be happy to give you a reference:
H. Klaus Johannsen, Alster Wohndesign, Tel. (040) 73983145.

4206 ______________________________

____

7 Phone calls on the job ▸ p. 70 • WB (p. 66) 12

Listen to four short phone calls. Match the calls with the descriptions below. There are two descriptions more than you need. Write the number of the call (1–4) in the correct box.

Der Anrufer/Die Anruferin ...

• möchte sich für einen Fehler entschuldigen.	
• möchte ein Datum für ein Treffen festlegen.	
• möchte eine Ankunftszeit mitteilen.	
• möchte die Gesprächspartnerin zum Essen einladen.	
• möchte mit jemanden sprechen, der zurzeit in einer Besprechung ist.	1
4207 • möchte zurückgerufen werden.	

8 Looking after visitors

▸ p. 70 • WB (pp. 67–68)

a) Anton is now working at Amcom in Berlin. Today he has to welcome a US visitor, who has just arrived at reception. Which of the following could Anton use? Tick (✔) or cross (✘) the speech bubbles.

- Did you have a good flight? ✔
- You look tired. Didn't you sleep on the plane? ✘
- Welcome to Amcom. My name's Anton, but please call me Toni. ☐
- How's the weather in New York at the moment? ☐
- Hello, Ms Wilson? Nice to meet you. ☐
- Is this your first visit to Berlin? ☐
- Our cafeteria on the top floor has excellent coffee. Would you like to go for coffee now? ☐
- We can have lunch in our canteen. It's not very good, but it's cheap. ☐
- Mr Schmidt asked me to show you round, but there isn't much to see, I'm afraid. ☐
- Mr Schmidt asked me to show you round. ☐

4308 *b) Write a short dialogue between Anton and Ms Wilson in your exercise book. Use some of the phrases you ticked (✔) in a) in a suitable order.*

9 Saying goodbye to visitors

▸ p. 70 • WB (pp. 67–68) 🎧 13

After the conference, Anton says goodbye to the visitor from New York. Choose phrases from the box to complete the dialogue. Then check with your CD (🎧 13).

> And I hope you had time to do some sightseeing. • Would you like me to call you a cab to the airport? • *I hope you had a good meeting.* • It was nice meeting you. Have a good flight. • OK, so your cab will be here in a few minutes.

Anton *I hope you had a good meeting.*

Ms Wilson Yes, we did. Successful and enjoyable, thank you.

Anton ____________________

Ms Wilson Well, I didn't have time for the city tour, but, well, next time maybe.

Anton ____________________

Ms Wilson Oh, yes, thank you. That would be great.

Anton ____________________

Ms Wilson Thank you, Toni. See you again next time maybe.

4309 *Anton* Goodbye. ____________________

LISTENING

In this part of your workbook you will find exercises that will help you prepare for exams.

1 Holidays (Listening for gist) ▸ *WB (p. 66)* 14

Look at the pictures. Then listen to five students. What kind of holidays do they like? Match the speakers to the pictures. Write the numbers of the speakers (1–5) in the boxes.

2 Talking about problems (Listening for gist) ▸ *WB (p. 66)* 15

Listen to four teenagers talking about their problems. Who is talking about what? Match the number of the speaker to the problem. There is one more than you need.

- Speaker 1 …
- Speaker 2 …
- Speaker 3 …
- Speaker 4 …

- wants to dump a friend.
- heard a friend say something that wasn't true.
- knows that someone fancies her boyfriend.
- is bad at school and can't tell his/her dad.
- gave a friend money and needs it back now.

3 Numbers, times, dates, letters (Listening for detail) ▸ WB (p. 66) 16–19

a) You will hear numbers, dates and telephone numbers. Listen (16) and mark what you hear: one of each pair.

14 / 40	15 / 50	160 / 116	347 / 374
1945 / 1954	2018 / 2080	0145500341 / 0144500341	06625330 / 06629330

b) Listen (17) and write the numbers, dates and telephone numbers (in figures, not words).

1 16 ____ 5 ____
2 ____ 6 ____
3 ____ 7 ____
4 ____ 8 ____

Tip
1 Listen for the endings '-een' and '-y', as in *16* and *60*.
2 You say numbers and years differently:
- **1984 (number)**: one thousand nine hundred and eighty-four.
- **1984 (year)**: nineteen eighty-four.

c) Listen (18) and write the time in figures.

1 7.30 ____ 2 ____ 3 ____ 4 ____

d) Which letters of the alphabet do you hear (19)?

4503 1 G ____ 2 ____ 3 ____ 4 ____ 5 ____ 6 ____

4 Announcements (Listening for detail) ▸ WB (p. 66) 20

Listen to the airport announcements and tick the correct box.

	True	False	Not given
1 Flight PS502 to Kiev has been cancelled[1] because of bad weather.	☐	☐	☐
2 The flight number for Glasgow is BE2958.	☐	☐	☐
3 The gate number has been changed for passengers[2] to Glasgow.	☐	☐	☐
4 The flight to Glasgow is delayed[3].	☐	☐	☐
5 The flight to Edinburgh is boarding[4] at Gate 30.	☐	☐	☐
6 There is a 15-minute delay on the flight to Chicago.	☐	☐	☐
7 The flight toToronto will leave at half past twelve.	☐	☐	☐
4504 8 The Toronto flight is delayed by about 45 minutes.	☐	☐	☐

5 Shopping (Listening for gist and detail) ▸ WB (p. 66) 21

a) Listen (21)[4] to two US teenagers, Beth and Amy. Where are they? Tick a box.

At a street market. ☐ In a department store. ☐ In a shoe shop. ☐

b) Listen again. What did the girls buy? Tick a box.

- ▸ A top and a pair of black jeans. ☐
- ▸ Two tops and a pair of white jeans. ☐
- 4505 ▸ Two tops and a pair of blue shorts. ☐

Tip
In informal speech (especially AE), expect to hear shortened forms, missing verbs and verb forms like ***gonna*** *(going to)*, ***wanna*** *(want to)*, ***dunno*** *(don't know)*, ***gotta*** *(have got to)*, ***kinda*** *(kind of)*.

[1]cancelled ['kænsld] *gestrichen* [2]passenger ['pæsɪndʒə] *Passagier, Reisende/r* [3]delayed [dɪ'leɪd] *verspätet*
[4]boarding ['bɔːdɪŋ] *hier: bereit zum Einsteigen* [5]fitting room ['fɪtɪŋ ˌruːm] *Anprobe*

6 Where are they from? (Accents) ▸ WB (p. 66) 22

Listen to six teenagers talking about sightseeing in London. Are they British, American or Australian? Write UK, US or Australia under the pictures.

4606

1 US | 2 ______ | 3 ______ | 4 ______ | 5 ______ | 6 ______

7 AE and BE ▸ WB (p. 66) 23

Listen to the US words. Find the British equivalents[1] in the box and write them next to the correct numbers.

film • flat • chips • underground • trousers • crisps • rubbish • city centre • holiday • timetable • pavement • mobile • ground floor • rubber • rucksack • biscuits • petrol station • lift • queue

1 film
2 ______
3 ______
4 ______
5 ______
6 ______
4607 7 ______

8 ______
9 ______
10 ______
11 ______
12 ______
13 ______
14 ______

Tip

Compare the main pronunciation differences of BE and AE:

	BE	AE
last, ask	[ɑː]	[æ]
clock, hot	[ɒ]	[ʌ]
new, Tuesday	[juː]	[uː]
here, shirt, park >	In AE you hear the 'r'.	
city, better, writer >	In AE 't' in the middle of a word sounds like 'd'.	

8 A first job (Fast speech) ▸ WB (p. 66) 24

a) *Listen to Mike and Terry talking about Terry's job. What do they talk about? Tick the correct boxes.*

A The working hours.
B The pay.
C The boss.
D The kind of work.

b) *What does Terry do at work? Tick the correct boxes.*

A Serve petrol.
B Take money.
C Serve customers.
D Fill the shelves.
4608 E Clean the toilet.
F Answer the phone.

[1]equivalent [ɪˈkwɪvələnt] *Entsprechung, entsprechendes Wort*

c) Are the following statements true or false? Listen again and tick the correct box.

	True	False	Not given
1 Terry works on Saturdays and Sundays.	☐	☐	☐
2 He works at a self-service[1] garage.	☐	☐	☐
3 He had worked at a supermarket checkout[2] before.	☐	☐	☐
4 There are lots of phone calls from customers on Saturdays.	☐	☐	☐
5 His shift is six hours long.	☐	☐	☐
6 Three assistants work in the shop for each shift.	☐	☐	☐
7 Terry doesn't like Alice and Barry very much.	☐	☐	☐
8 Terry is 17 years old.	☐	☐	☐

9 Teen work and pay in the UK (Listening for detail) ▸ *WB (p. 66)* 25

a) Read the questions before you listen. Then listen and tick the correct box(es) to complete the sentences. Sometimes 2 of 3 boxes are correct. Check your answers when you listen a second time.

Tip

In **multiple-choice** tasks read the task first and look for the **key words**: the different ages and 'school holidays'. Numbers are always important, so listen carefully.

1 If you're 13,
- ☐ you can work for two hours on school days.
- ☐ you can work in a factory.
- ☐ you can work for two hours before school.

2 If you're 14,
- ☐ you can work 12 hours a week during term time.
- ☐ you can do all kinds of work.
- ☐ you can't work in a factory.

3 In the school holidays, if you're 13 or 14,
- ☐ you can work 5 hours on weekdays and Saturdays.
- ☐ you are allowed to work 25 hours a week altogether.
- ☐ you aren't allowed to work on Sundays.

4 In the school holidays, if you're 15 or 16,
- ☐ you can work 35 hours a week.
- ☐ you can work all day on Sundays.
- ☐ you can work between 10 pm and 6 am.

b) Listen again and answer the questions in a few words.

1 What's the name of the radio programme? ______

2 What's the programme about today? ______

3 What is the school-leaving age in the UK? ______

4 What kind of work are 13-year-olds allowed to do? ______

5 How many hours a day can you work at age 13? ______

6 How many hours a week can you work at age 14? ______

7 How many hours can you work on Saturdays at 14? ______

8 How many hours can 15- and 16-year-olds work on Saturdays? ______

9 How old must you be to get the National Minimum Wage[3]? ______

10 How much is the NMW if you're 16 or 17? ______

Tip

Look for **key words** in the sentences and mark them.
Numbers are always important, so listen carefully. Listen exactly for phrases that are almost the same: 'hours a day' or 'hours a week'?

[1]self-service [ˌself ˈsɜːvɪs] *Selbstbedienung* [2]checkout [ˈtʃekaʊt] *Kasse* [3]National Minimum Wage [weɪdʒ] *staatlich vorgeschriebener Mindestlohn*

10 A radio phone-in (Listening for detail) ▸ WB (p. 66) 26

You will hear a radio phone-in about young people and their families. Read the tasks first, then listen and tick the correct answer: A, B or C.

1 The phone-in programme is about …
- A divorced people.
- B single-parent families.
- C patchwork families.

2 Mark lives with …
- A his stepdad.
- B his dad.
- C his mum and his sister in Scotland.

3 Jan is …
- A Mark's stepsister.
- B Mark's mother.
- C Mark's sister.

4 Marie has got …
- A one stepsister and one stepbrother.
- B two stepbrothers and a stepsister.
- C three stepbrothers.

5 Sharon is …
- A Marie's stepmother.
- B Marie's stepsister.
- C Marie's mum.

6 David's dad lives in …
- A London.
- B Sydney.
- C San Francisco.

7 David is from …
- A the UK.
- B the USA.
- C Australia.

8 David lives …
- A with his father and stepmother.
- B with his mother and stepfather.
- C in Sydney.

9 Nicole's dad lives in …
- A Coventry.
- B Oxford.
- C Poland.

10 Nicole has got …
- A a stepsister in Poland.
- B a stepbrother in Poland.
- C a brother in Poland.

Tip

Read the **answers A–C carefully** before you listen. If you are not sure the first time, write '?', then complete the missing answers when you listen again.

[1]step- [step] *Stief-*

SPEAKING

11 Describing pictures

▸ SF (pp. 125–126) • WB (pp. 67–68) 27

a) Look carefully at the picture. Collect words to describe the scene: action, people, background, atmosphere. If you don't know the words you need, look them up in a dictionary.

Scene: *school sports day, end of school year, athletics,* ______________

____

People/actions: *parents, family, teachers,* ______________

runners: wear, run, win, ______________

Atmosphere/feelings: *excited,* ______________

____

b) Prepare to speak for two minutes about the picture. Use vocabulary from a). Write notes.

- Describe the scene. Say where it is and what's happening.
  The picture shows a scene in summer … The weather is …. Maybe the picture shows the school sports day …
- Describe the people, say how many there are, what they are doing/wearing, what they are probably speaking about. Use the following: ***on the right/left, in the middle/centre/background/foreground, at the top/bottom of the picture, at the front/back: behind, in front of, over, under, on, next to, between***
  We see students, parents, … The parents seem to be … The girl/boy at the front/back …
- Say what the people are probably feeling/thinking:
  He/She might be thinking (that) … I expect the parents are feeling …

Tip

Don't **answer** questions with only *yes* or *no*.
Say: *Yes, I do. /Yes, I am. / No, I don't./ No, I'm not./ No, I don't think so,* etc.

If you repeat an idea or opinion, try to say it with different words.

c) Prepare to answer questions which have to do with the picture indirectly, for example questions about sports or competitions. Listen to the questions on your CD (27) and prepare two or three sentences for each answer. Make notes first. Practise your answers with and without your notes.

12 Asking about and giving opinions ▸ WB (pp. 67–68) • GF 2 (p. 151)

a) *Look carefully at the picture.*

b) *Use phrases from box 1 to write four questions that you could ask a partner about the picture.*

1 What/Why do you think …?	What's your opinion about …?
What is …?	What should … do?
Do you agree that …?	What advice would you give?

Why do you think the bullies are hitting the younger boy?

c) *Use phrases from box 2 to give your opinion on what is happening in the picture. What do you think the boy could/should do now and in future? Give advice.*

2 In my opinion,, …	I can't imagine …
I (dis)agree (that) …	I don't think people know …
I really don't think …	My advice would be to …
I feel/believe (that) …	I think he/she should/ought to …
I don't think … would be a good idea …	The problem seems to be that …

In my opinion, bullies always have big problems.

5012
5013

13 Comparing pictures

▸ SF (pp. 125–126) • WB (pp. 67–68)

Think of arguments for and against having a weekend job or learning for exams at the weekend. Make notes.

Doing a weekend job	Learning for school at the weekend
For	**For**
Against	**Against**

b) *Talk about the advantages and disadvantages. Practise speaking first with your notes, then without them.*

14 Talking about cartoons

▸ SF (p. 126) • WB (pp. 67–68)

Talk about the cartoon using ideas/phrases from the box and your own ideas.

1. Describe what you see and what the people are doing.
2. What's the cartoonist's message? Is it clear?
3. Give your opinion on the cartoon. Do you like it?

The cartoon shows the problem of ...
We see the mother at ... The son is sitting at ...
The son tells the mother that ...

The cartoonist wants to say that teenagers ...
communicate – use electronic media too much –
talk to family less

I like/don't like the cartoon because ...

WRITING

15 Writing better sentences 1 (Using adjectives and adverbs) ▸ WB (p. 68)

Look again at the picture story on p. 16 of your workbook. Complete the sentences with words from the boxes.

Adjectives
funny • brown • good-looking • interesting • old • small • sporty • terrible • blond

Adverbs and adverb phrases
excitedly • loudly • luckily • quickly • suddenly • one day • the next day • in the next town • on the way

Picture 1: One day Anna suddenly received a text from her boyfriend, Tom. ______ she read his message. He had dumped her! She was shocked and couldn't believe it.

Tip
Adjectives (*good, excited*) and **adverbs** (*well, excitedly*) make your texts more interesting. Use them as much as possible.

Picture 2: Anna called her best friend for advice. Her friend told her not to sit at home.

Picture 3: So Anna called her cousin and decided to visit her for the weekend.

Picture 4: ______, Anna ______ packed her rucksack and left on her ______ moped. The weather was just the way she felt – ______. It was raining.

Picture 5: ______ she stopped at a ______ café ______.
She didn't notice that a ______ young guy with ______ hair had just come in.

Picture 6: The young guy sat down at the next table. He was wearing a ______ jacket and jeans. He started an ______ conversation about mopeds and told Anna a ______ story about his moped that made her laugh. They chatted and laughed a lot.

Picture 7: Anna and the young guy left the café together, talking ______. ______, it had stopped raining. They would meet again the next day. Tom? Who was Tom? Had she forgotten him already?

5215

16 Writing better sentences 2 (Using linking words) ▸ WB (p. 68)

a) Mark the correct word.

1 (When/If) Dominic and Afra get married next week, it will be a Muslim wedding.

2 (Because/Although) there are some disadvantages of mixed relationships, there are also many advantages.

3 Sometimes a relationship doesn't work (so that/because) the different religions make life difficult.

4 Sometimes the partners don't know much about each other's religion, (so/so that) they are not tolerant enough.

5 Sometimes one partner changes to the religion of the other, (but/so that) there are no problems.

Tip

Use **linking words** in your written texts for a better style. Remember the word order after the linking word: Subject-Verb-Object. *Partners can be happy* ***although*** *they have different religions.*

b) Choose words from the box to complete the sentences.

after • because • so • so ... that • ~~when~~

1 When ________ young people fall in love, they often don't care about religion.

2 Problems in mixed relationships usually start ________ the couple have lived together for some time.

3 Sometimes the partners don't know much about each other's religion, ________ they are not tolerant enough.

4 Sometimes one partner changes to the religion of the other, ________ they have the same religion.

5316
5317
5 Mixed relationships often work well ________ the partners respect each other's religion.

17 Correcting mistakes ▸ WB (p. 69)

Correct this e-mail from Lotte to her cousin in the UK. Find 14 mistakes, mark them and correct them in the space below.

Tip

Make a **check list** of your 'favourite mistakes' and look for them when you read through your text. Look for:
- spelling
- verb tenses
- word order
- *do/does/did*
- uncountable nouns (*information*)
- articles (*the, a/an*).

Hi Becca!
Here I am at last! Sorry I didn't write to you since Christmas. I've been at home with a very bad cold since a week. I had a temperature too, so the doctor said I must to stay in the bed, but tomorrow I go to school again. My best news are that I am going to do volunteer work after school, maybe in Indien for six months. My teacher gave me some advices, and I have got a lot of informations from the internet. Our neighbour's daughter also went to India last year, and she has done some really intresting work in a school. I would like to work on an environmental[1] project. Mum has told to me that you did volunteer work after you left school. What did you? I'm already looking forward on seeing you all again. I'm sure we'll have a great time. I hope the whether will be good. If not, we can go shoping. OK. That's enough for today. I call you again soon, maybe next weekend.
Love to everybody,
Lotte

Correct

I haven't written, for a week, I had to,
____
____

5318

[1]environmental [ɪn,vaɪrən'mentl] *Umwelt-*

18 Writing a text (Collecting and organizing ideas)

▸ SF (p. 140, 146)

a) Staying at home is better than going on holiday in summer.
*Decide if you agree or disagree with the statement. Collect more ideas **for** or **against**. Then read the tip and write your finished list in your exercise book. Look up useful words and phrases that you will need..*

Tip

Brainstorming:
1. Write down **all** your ideas, even if they don't seem very useful.
2. Then read your list and **cross out** the ideas that you won't use.
3. **Order** the good ideas and **number** them.

Notes/Ideas: **'Spending the summer holidays at home is the best thing.'**

For:
- stay in bed longer
- enjoy sun and outdoors
- do work experience
- hang out every day
- do hobbies
- enough time to read
- sit at the computer longer
- watch TV and DVDs
- do cycle tours
- help parents
- work on a volunteer project

Against:
- friends are often not at home
- weather often not good
- boring, nothing to do
- parents at work
- have to look after younger brothers/sisters
- swimming pools full
- a lot of places are closed for holidays
- have to tidy your room
- have to help at home

*b) Use the ideas **for** or **against** in a) to write a text of about 100 words in your exercise book.*

Your text should have three main parts: beginning, middle *and* end.

1 beginning: Introduce your topic with a general sentence or with a sentence about your own experience. For example:

All school students love the summer holidays. Sometimes families go on holiday to a hot country. But I think staying at home is good too because ...

2 middle: Write about things you can do, things you don't have to do. Give examples. Use a new paragraph for each new idea.

First, ... Second, ... Finally, ... For example, ... One reason is ...

For example:

First, you can do all the things that you can't do in term time. For example, you can go to bed later and sleep longer. This means that you can ...

3 end: Sum up your thoughts and write a short conclusion. For example:

To sum up, I think that it is better to stay at home in the summer holidays because ... In conclusion, I agree that ... because ...

19 Writing a report (The 5 Ws + how) ▸ WB (pp. 68–69)

A good text gives the reader important information in the first few sentences: ***who*** *the text is about,* ***what*** *happened or took place,* ***where, when*** *and* ***why*** *it happened and sometimes* ***how*** *it happened. The order is not always the same.*

a) *Read the following text about John Lennon. Then write the information which answers the* ***5 Ws*** *and* ***how***.

On 8th December 1980 at 10.50 pm the founder[1] of the *Beatles*, John Lennon, was murdered by Mark David Chapman. Lennon was shot in the back four times with a revolver. The shooting took place in NYC, in front of the exclusive apartment house, the Dakota Building, on West 72nd Street, where Lennon and his wife lived. At the time of the killing the motive was unclear, but Chapman had a history of mental illness.

When: *8th December 1980 at 10.50 pm*

Who: __________

What: __________

Where: __________

Why: __________

How: __________

b) *Now read a reporter's notes about an accident. Then use the notes to write the newspaper report.*

NOTES
boy, 13, on bike, doing paper round before school, hit by car, yesterday at about 7.20 am, Willow Road Merton, black Toyota Auris driving too fast, wet road – couldn't stop, boy crossed road without looking, St. Mary's hospital, broken leg and shock

Accident report

A thirteen-year-old boy on a bicycle was hit by a car when he was doing his paper round before school. The accident happened __________

c) *Write a short text about the wedding[2] of Robbie Williams. Give information on the 5 Ws and add a few details from below to add interest. Write in your exercise book.*

- Robbie Williams, the best-selling UK solo artist, married Turkish-American actress Ayda Field at his luxury villa in Beverly Hills, Los Angeles
- Saturday 7th August 2010 at 5 pm
- at a private party with only family and close friends
- the ceremony[3] was simple but beautiful
- they met in 2006
- Ayda was 31 and Robbie was 36 when they married
- he asked her to marry him on the telephone
- *Take That* could not go to the wedding because they were all on holiday
- the wedding plans were kept secret[4]

[1]founder [ˈfaʊndə] *Gründer* [2]wedding [ˈwedɪŋ] *Hochzeit* [3]ceremony [ˈserəˌmɒni] *hier: Trauung* [4]secret [ˈsiːkrət] *geheim*

READING

20 Doing your own thing ▸ WB (pp. 66–67)

a) Before you read, skim the text and mark the correct answer, A, B or C.

The text …

- A gives information to parents.
- B describes a typical teenage problem.
- C is about bullying.

Do your own thing – what *you* want, not what *they* want!

Tip

To get a first impression of the topic of the text, look at the **title**, **headings**, **picture(s)**, and words in **bold** type.

Doing your own thing

Who are your peers[1]?

Your peers are the people around you, people of your age, for example your classmates, the people in your sports team, kids at your youth club or in the neighbourhood.

What is peer pressure[2]?

Young people are sometimes persuaded to do things (or not to do things) by their peers. If their peers are doing it, they feel that they should do it too. It isn't easy to be the only one who's different. But the things that their peers persuade them to do may be good or bad.

Positive peer pressure

If your peers have a healthy attitude, for example to school, they can motivate you to do your best and use your potential. They may persuade you to join a sports club or an environmental[3] group, things which can influence you in a positive way.

Negative peer pressure

Your peers can also influence you negatively. They can persuade you to do things that are bad for you. Typical examples are drinking alcohol, smoking at an early age, missing school without permission[4], even taking drugs. They may want you to do things that are also bad for others, even dangerous or illegal things. This could be bullying, shoplifting, vandalism, joining a gang or even carrying a knife.

Why do young people do what others want?

People give in to peer pressure because they want to be accepted by the peer group. They want to fit in. They are afraid of losing 'friends'. They think their peers will laugh at them or bully them if they say No. Often they are 'dared' to do something wrong or illegal – like stealing. They want to show that they are not afraid or they want to impress the group leader. Very often they end up in trouble with the law, or sometimes in hospital. Often the peers don't even care …

It is not always easy to say No to peers. Going against your peers takes a lot of courage[5] and a strong character.

What you can do

Be critical. Choose your friends carefully. Spend time with peers who basically share your views. It's better to have one really good friend than a whole group who just want to control you. Do only what you feel is right. Don't do things you might regret, just because others want you to. If you are unsure, talk to an older teen, a brother or sister. Being strong will give you self-confidence, and true friends will respect you even more.

5801

[1]peer [pɪə] *deinesgleichen, Gleichaltrige* [2]peer pressure ['pɪə ˌpreʃə] *Druck/ Einfluss der Clique* [3]environmental [ɪnˌvaɪrən'mentl] *Umwelt-* [4]permission [pə'mɪʃn] *Erlaubnis* [5]courage ['kʌrɪdʒ] *Mut*

b) Match and complete the sentences with the correct ending. Write a letter (A–E) in the boxes below.

1 Your peers can influence you …
2 Peers who are good friends can …
3 When your peers pressure[1] you, you should …
4 If you can say No, you show …
5 Teenagers sometimes give in to peer pressure because …

A motivate you to do positive things.
B do what you feel is right.
C in a positive or negative way.
D they want to be accepted by their peers.
E that you have a strong character.

1 C 2 ☐ 3 ☐ 4 ☐ 5 ☐

c) Complete the sentences with information from the text. Write in your exercise book. Use your own words as much as possible.

1 Your peers are …
2 Positive peer pressure means …
3 Peer pressure is often negative. For example, …
4 There are a few reasons why young people do what their peers do. For example, …
5 You can show you have a strong character if you …

Tip
Scan the text and look for **key words**. Then read around them to find the answer.

21 Working out the meaning of words ▸ WB (p. 66)

Look at the text in exercise 20 again. How did you work out the meaning of the words that are new? Write the words below in the lists with their German meaning. Some words fit in two lists. Decide what helped you most.

persuade • motivate • potential • influence • shoplifting • impress • critical • fit in • dare • regret • self-confidence • unsure

From the context	Like a German word	From a part of the word or from the word family
persuade – überreden	motivate – motivieren	shoplifting – Ladendiebstahl

[1]pressure [ˈpreʃə] *auf jdn. Druck ausüben*

22 What do UK teenagers think? ▸ *WB (pp. 66–67)*

a) Skim the text. What does it report? Mark A, B or C.

A Teenagers' problems with family and others.
B Mainly negative things about British teenagers.
C Mainly positive things about British teenagers.

Britain's teenagers: What do they think?

Teens are not always popular with adults or the media. Many people think they are lazy, noisy troublemakers who do not respect adults. People often think teenagers just want to have fun. But this seems to be true only for a minority of teenagers. Surveys[1] which asked teens about their attitudes found that they have quite old-fashioned views.

Family values[2]

- Over 90% of UK teenagers believe in marriage.
- Six out of ten teenagers think it is better to get married before having children.
- Two-thirds think that too many teenage pregnancies are terminated[3].
- 8,000 under 16s become pregnant every year, and 40,000 under 18s. Teenage birth rates in Britain are twice as high as in Germany and six times higher than in Holland.
- The survey *Typical Young People* found that most teenagers have respect for their parents and usually listen to what they have to say.
- 70% of teenagers say that their parents let them make their own decisions.
- Two-thirds of teenage girls see their mother as their role model[4], not a female media star.
- When boys were asked about their role models, three times more named their father as a role model, not footballers or rappers.
- Young people do not want to have an extravagant lifestyle like many media stars. Most teenagers just want enough money to be financially independent.

Social values

- A 2010 survey on *International Citizenship* found that most British teens have democratic and tolerant views. They expect to vote[5] in future but will not join a political party.
- Teens in Britain care about their community and the environment[6]. They are interested, even if they are not active.
- Over 80% have a strong sense[7] of national identity and are proud to be British.

6003

[1]survey ['sɜːveɪ] *Umfrage* [2]values ['væljuːz] *Werte* [3]terminated ['tɜːmɪneɪtɪd] *beendet* [4]role model ['rəʊl ˌmɒdl] *Vorbild* [5]vote [vəʊt] *wählen* [6]environment [ɪnˌvaɪrənmənt] *Umwelt* [7]sense [sens] *Sinn*

b) Read the statements below. Are they true or false? Write T or F.

Tip
Look for **key words** in the statements and mark them before you read the text.
There are other ways of talking about numbers.
For example:
70% = 7 out of 10
66% = two-thirds
75% = three-quarters
over = more than
under = less/fewer than.

1 Some people think that teenagers in the UK show little respect for adults. T
2 Surveys find that the statement in 1) may be true.
3 Fewer than 10% of British teenagers do not believe in marriage.
4 60% think it's better to be married before you start a family.
5 Holland has the highest rate of single teenage mothers.
6 Over 60% of teens think their mother has a positive influence[1] on them.
7 Teenagers think media stars make good role models.
8 Seven out of ten teenagers say their parents let them decide things themselves.
9 More than 20% of UK teenagers are not proud to be British.

c) Find and write statements from the text which mean the same as the following:

Tip
Look for words in the sentences and text that mean **the same**.
For example:
negative – bad
media – press
mom – mother.

1 Teens often have a bad reputation[2] and a bad press.

Teens are not always popular with adults or the media. (l. 2)

2 Less than ten percent of UK teens think that getting married is not important.

3 More than sixty percent of female teens say their mum is the person they look up to most.

4 British teenagers take an interest in community and environmental issues[3], even if they don't always play an active role.

[1]influence ['ɪnfluəns] *Einfluss* [2]reputation [ˌrepju'teɪʃn] *Ruf, Ansehen* [3]issue ['ɪʃuː] *Thema, Frage*

MEDIATION

23 Signs (Mediating from English to German) ▸ *WB (pp. 69–70)*

Du bist in England mit einem Freund, der nicht so gut Englisch kann. Er möchte wissen, was auf den Schildern steht. Erkläre ihm kurz auf Deutsch was man darf, nicht darf oder muss.

Tip

You don't have to understand all the words. Report the meaning in your **own words**. Leave out details and keep it simple. **Don't translate.**

(1) Please wait here to be seated[1].

Du musst hier warten. / Du darfst dich

(2) Self-service restaurant. Please do not wait to be served.

(3) Please leave your dog outside and your shopping trolley[2] inside!

(4) Please check your change before you leave the shop. No money back later!

5601

24 London for teens (Mediating from English to German) ▸ *WB (pp. 69–70)*

Berichte deinen Freunden auf Deutsch, was man in London alles sehen und erleben kann. Sie möchten Folgendes wissen:

- wo man gut und billig essen kann.
- wo man Aufregendes/Gruseliges erleben kann.
- wo man angesagte Kleidung preiswert kaufen kann.
- wie teuer Tickets für ein Musical sind.
- wo man toll abhängen kann.

Tip

Look for **key words**. Don't report details or opinions, only **facts** (places, prices).

There are some amazing attractions for teenage tourists in London. Here are just a few of them:
From the big wheel – called the **London Eye** – you have a fantastic view over the whole of London. Expensive – but worth[3] it. Long queues but great photos!
See the skeleton of a diplodocus dinosaur at the **Natural History Museum** – it's 26 m long!
If you like really scary places, try the **London Dungeon**[4]! Find out about London's dark and horrible history. Meet Jack the Ripper and the world-famous barber[5] Sweeney Todd. You're sure to have bad dreams! Open every day. In summer from 9.30–6.30 (16–29 July), 9.30–7pm (August), 10am–5.30 (Sept).
Hungry? If you like Indian and Bangladeshi food, try a curry at one of the many **Brick Lane** curry houses! The food is delicious and not expensive. Visit the weekend street market there for trendy young fashions and second-hand clothes too.
Camden Market (Saturdays and Sundays only) is the largest open-air market in the UK, with half a million visitors every week! It's a great place to hang out or to shop for trendy alternative fashions by young designers, fashion jewellery and antiques. You'll see designer workshops, exotic food stalls[6], cafés and bars – even famous people!
Don't miss a **West End** musical – *We Will Rock You, Chicago, The Lion King, The Phantom of the Opera* and many more! Tickets are not cheap, (from about £25 to £80), but go to Leicester Square and get tickets for the same day at half price!

[1]seat [siːt] *jdm. einen Platz zuweisen* [2]trolley ['trɒli] *Einkaufswagen* [3]worth [wɜːθ] *Wert* [4]dungeon ['dʌndʒən] *Kerker, Verlies*
[5]barber ['bɑːbə] *(Herren)Frisör* [6]stall [stɔːl] *Stand, Marktstand*

25 US film comedy 'You Again' (Mediating from English to German) ▸ WB (pp. 69–70)

You saw the US film comedy You Again (Du schon wieder) and want to tell the story to a friend. Use the English summary of part of the storyline to make notes in German. Don't translate.

US film comedy *You Again* (2010)

When Marni was in high school, she was ignored by the boys and bullied by the girls because of her acne and braces[1]. Her worst enemy was Joana, head of the cheerleading team. Now Marni has a successful job in New York, but she has not forgotten how unhappy her schooldays were. Marni goes back home to her brother Will's wedding, and discovers that he is going to get married to – Joana!

When the girls meet, Marni expects Joana to say sorry for the high school bullying, but Joana pretends[2] not to remember her. Marni tells Gail, her mother, about how Joana had bullied her in the past. Gail tells Marni to put it behind her because everybody deserves[3] a second chance. But Marni decides to protect her brother and show him what Joana is really like – before he makes a big mistake. But will her brother believe her?

26 Apprenticeships (Mediating from German to English) ▸ WB (pp. 69–70)

You have found these adverts for apprenticeships in your local newspaper. Write notes in English so that you can tell your English cousin about them in an e-mail. Tell her what qualifications you need and what kind of person they are looking for:

You have to have/be ...

Tip

Try to **paraphrase** words you don't know with simple words that you know. For example, *Hotelfachfrau/-mann: someone who is the manager of a hotel.*

1 Für unseren Betrieb in Hamburg suchen wir zum 01.08. Auszubildende zum
Mechaniker (in)
Sie haben gute Noten in Mathematik und Deutsch (Mittlere Reife) und ein gutes technisches Verständnis, sind teamfähig, lernbereit, flexibel, haben gute kommunikative Eigenschaften und Interesse am Kunden-Service. Wir bieten eine Ausbildung in einer modernen, gut ausgestatteten Werkstatt. Bewerbung bitte an H. Böhm, Schiller Motors.

2 Möchten Sie eine gesicherte Zukunft in der Residence Hotelkette?
Auszubildende/r Hotelfachfrau/-mann
ab 01.08. gesucht.
Wir erwarten einen guten Schulabschluss (Mittlere Reife) mit guten Noten in Mathe, Deutsch und Englisch. Ein absolviertes Praktikum in einem Hotel/Restaurant wäre von Vorteil. Bewerbung bitte schriftlich an Fr. Herold, Residence Hotel, Paul Klee ...

3 Gehobenes 4-Sterne Hotel in Hamburg su. ab sof.
auszubildende/n Köchin/Koch
für unsere moderne Großküche.
Sie sind freundlich, fleißig und teamfähig.
Praktikum in einer Hotelküche erwünscht aber nicht erforderlich.
Bewerbung telefonisch unter 040/401 6927.

4 Für Neueröffnung unseres Friseursalons im Zentrum Hamburgs suchen wir ab sofort
Auszubildende(m/w)
für unser junges Team
Sie sind kontaktfreudig, zuverlässig und arbeiten gern in einem Team. Kontaktaufnahme bitte unter 0173/624 8942 (H. Anders) od. schriftlich an Alster Haarmoden, Wagnerstr.

5704

[1]braces ['breɪsɪz] *Zahnspange* [2]pretend [prɪ'tend] *so tun als ob* [3]deserve [dɪ'zɜːv] *verdienen*

LANGUAGE

27 A postcard from San Francisco (Simple present or present progressive)

▸ WB (p. 70)

Simple present or present progressive? Underline the correct form of the verb to complete Marie's postcard:

Hi Sarah!

Surprise! Surprise! We ('re spending/spend) a week in San Francisco!

We (don't usually go/aren't usually going) on holiday at Easter, but Dad's American friend ('s living/lives) here. We ('re visiting/visit) his family for a week. We ('re loving/love) it here.♥Steve (doesn't like/is not liking) writing postcards, so at the moment he (takes/'s taking) photos. Every day we ('re seeing/see) something cool. We (don't often get/aren't often getting) lost. Someone always (helps/'s helping) us. We (have/'re having) a really great time – and we (aren't missing/don't miss) dirty old Liverpool! Will be home next week. ☹

Love, Marie

6201

Tip

Use the **simple present** with *often, usually, never, always, every day* and verbs such as *like, love, know, believe, seem, look, see*.

Use the **present progressive** with *now, at the moment, today*.

28 A questionnaire (Question forms)

▸ GF 2 (p. 151)

Put the words in the correct order and write the questions for a questionnaire in English on free-time activities.

QUESTIONNAIRE ON FREE-TIME ACTIVITIES

1 the computer/use/**Do**/every day/you — *Do you use the computer every day?*

2 hours/**How many**/at/spend/do/the computer/you/every day — *How many hours do you spend at the computer every day?*

3 a/phone/got/mobile/you/**Have** ____________

4 every day/many/you/make/do/calls/**On average**/how ____________

5 like/best/sports/do/**Which**/you ____________

6 music/like/do/**What kind of**/you ____________

7 a rock concert/you/ever/been/**Have**/to ____________

8 on holiday/you/**Did**/go/last year ____________

9 did/**Where**/go/you ____________

10 with friends/you/ever/**Have**/on holiday/been ____________

6202
6203

29 A true romance (Simple past or past progressive) ▸ WB (pp. 70–71)

Simple past or past progressive? Underline the correct verb form in brackets.

The couple (met/were meeting) in September 2001 when they (studied/were studying) art history in their first year at University in Scotland. HE first (was noticing/noticed) how attractive SHE was when SHE (modelled/was modelling) clothes for a university fashion show. In their second year, they (shared/were sharing) a house with friends. They (didn't talk/weren't talking) about their relationship. The press (wasn't finding out/didn't find out) about it until 2004, while the couple (spent/were spending) a skiing holiday in Switzerland. Paparazzi (photographed/were photographing) HER with HIM and HIS father when they (queued/were queueing) at a ski lift. In 2007 they (were breaking up/broke up) but got back together again some months later. While HE (was doing/did) military service in the RAF[1], SHE (didn't work/wasn't working). That (didn't please/wasn't pleasing) HIS grandmother, so SHE quickly (was looking/looked) for a job. The couple finally (was marrying/married) on 29th April 2011 – and now she doesn't need a job. Who are they?

6303

Tip

Use the **simple past** to report **when** something happened in the past.
Use the **past progressive** to say **what** was happening at a time in the past, often with *while, just when, as*.

30 WORDS Describing people

a) Complete the sentences with a suitable word from the box.

arrogant • bossy • easy-going • *good-looking* • honest • jealous • reliable • romantic • shy

1 Vicky's new boyfriend is very *good-looking* but he knows it and he's a bit ________.

2 Sandra's boyfriend doesn't like it when she talks to other boys. He gets ________.

3 The new girl is ________. She likes to tell everybody what to do.

4 Tom isn't very ________. He's often late for work and he forgets things.

5 I'm sure that what my brother says is true. He's always ________.

6 Don't be ________ at the interview. Smile and look confident.

7 I like friends who are relaxed and ________, not too serious.

8 Charlotte's boyfriend isn't very ________. He always takes her to football matches and horror films.

b) Put the adjectives from a) into two groups: positive and negative. Then find more adjectives to describe people for each group. You can use your Dictionary in your student's book (pp. 173–203).

☺ *good-looking,* ________

____

☹ *arrogant,* ________

____

6304

[1]RAF = Royal Air Force

31 WORDS Hobbies and free-time activities

a) *Choose words from the box that go with the verbs below. Sometimes there's more than one.*

cartoons • computer games • cards • cycling • DVDs • e-mails • *judo* • *karate* • magazines • models • music • out • photos • riding • shopping • *sport* • swimming • the guitar • the net

do judo, karate, sport ______

draw ______

go ______

hang ______

listen to ______

6405 make ______

play ______

read ______

surf ______

take ______

watch ______

write ______

b) *Write four sentences about what you do and when you usually do it.*

I usually hang out with friends on Saturdays.

______

______

______

______

______

32 Explaining words (Paraphrasing) ▸ *WB (p. 68)*

If you don't know the English word for what you want to say, you can paraphrase it. Paraphrasing is useful in mediation. Choose some of these phrases to paraphrase the words below:

It's like ... ***It's the same as/similar to ...***
It's someone who ... ***It's something that ...***
It's a place where ... ***It's a (use a general word like 'school') that ...***

Tip

Use words that you know, with details to make the meaning clear. Keep your sentences **simple**.

1 Internat: *It's a private school where students live during the school term.*

2 gelähmt: *It's similar to 'disabled', when*

3 Handlung (eines Films): ______

4 Abenteuerfilm: ______

5 (Film-)Rezensent/in: ______

______

6 Kino: ______

33 WORDS Word families

Complete the chart. Then complete the sentences with the correct words in the correct form.

verb	noun	adjective
______	application	–
argue	argument	–
compare	______	–
decide	______	–
explain	______	–
organize	______	______
–	success	______
–	______	strong

I've ______ for a job. I can't ______ what to wear for the interview tomorrow. – At an interview they often ask you about your ______ and weaknesses. Even if you don't agree with the interviewer, don't ______ with him or her! Good luck! I hope you' ll be ______.

6507

34 Dating (Prepositions)

Choose and underline the correct word.

1 Could you ever fall in love (with/in) a person much older than you?
2 I would never date anyone I met (in/on) the internet, because I wouldn't know enough (about/over) them.
3 Kelly has dumped her boyfriend. She said they were too different (of/from) each other.
4 She said he never stopped talking (about/of) football and she was fed up (of/with) it.
5 (After/In) my opinion, she did the right thing. You can't stay (by/with) a person like that.

6508

35 WORDS Opposites

a) Find and write pairs of opposites.

boring • dry • fat • hard-working • majority • outdoor • relaxed • simple • soft • thin • well

badly • complicated • *exciting* • hard • indoor • lazy • minority • nervous • skinny • thick • wet

boring – exciting	______	______
______	______	______
______	______	______
______	______	______

b) Write four sentences in your exercise book. Use a pair of opposites from a) in each sentence.

6509 *My friend said the film was boring, but I thought that it was exciting.*

LISTENING SKILLS

SF Listening ► *p. 132*

Was muss ich beim *listening* beachten?

Vor dem Hören:

- Überlege, worum es in dem Hörtext gehen wird. Frag dich, was du schon über das Thema weißt.
- Lies die Aufgaben gut durch, damit du weißt, worauf du achten sollst:
  - auf die **Hauptgedanken** oder die **Kernaussage** des Textes, z. B. wenn du sagen sollst, um welches Thema es geht, oder welche Meinung der Sprecher zu dem Thema hat.
  - auf bestimmte **Details**, z. B. wenn du Namen, Uhrzeiten, Jahreszahlen heraushören sollst.
- Bereite dich darauf vor, Notizen zu machen. Leg z. B. eine Tabelle oder Liste an.

Beim Hören:

- Keine Panik! Du musst nicht alles verstehen. Konzentriere dich auf das Wesentliche. Oft werden wichtige Informationen wiederholt.
- Achte auf Geräusche und unterschiedliche Stimmen. Was ein Sprecher/eine Sprecherin besonders betont, das ist wichtig!
- Wenn du gezielt nach Informationen suchst, denk an die Aufgabe und lass dich von anderen Einzelheiten nicht ablenken. Aufgepasst: die Informationen, die du suchst, kommen vielleicht in einer anderen Reihenfolge vor, als du sie erwartest.
- Manche Signalwörter machen es dir leichter, den Hörtext zu verstehen:
  Aufzählung: **and**, **another**, **too** / Gegensatz: **although**, **but** / Grund, Folge: **because**, **so**, **so that** / Vergleich: **larger/older/... than**, **more**, **most** / Reihenfolge: **before**, **after**, **then**, **next**, **later**, **when**, **at last**, **at the same time**.
- Mache kurze Notizen, z. B. Anfangsbuchstaben, Symbole oder Stichworte.

Nach dem Hören:

- Vervollständige deine Notizen sofort.
- Konzentriere dich beim zweiten Hören auf das, was du beim ersten Mal nicht gut verstanden hast.

READING COURSE

Working out the meaning of words ► *p. 134*

Was hilft dir, unbekannte Wörter zu verstehen?

1. **Bilder** zeigen oft die Dinge, die du im Text nicht verstehst. Wenn es Bilder zum Text gibt, dann schau sie dir vor dem Lesen genau an.
2. Oft hilft dir der **Textzusammenhang *(context)***, z. B. *When we* ***reached*** *the station, Judy went to the ticket machine to buy our tickets.*
3. Manche englischen Wörter werden **ähnlich wie im Deutschen** geschrieben oder ausgesprochen, z. B. **excellent**, **millionaire**, **nation**, **reality**.
4. Manchmal stecken in unbekannten Wörtern **bekannte Teile**, z. B. **friendliness**, **helpless**, **understandable**, **gardener**, **tea bag**, **waiting room**.

Skimming and scanning ► *p. 134*

Skimming: Lesen, um sich einen Überblick zu verschaffen

Beim **Skimming** überfliegst du einen Text schnell, um dir einen ersten **Überblick** zu verschaffen, worum es geht. Du willst z. B. herausfinden, ob ein Text (im Internet oder in einem Buch) überhaupt nützliche Informationen zu deinem Thema (z. B. für ein Referat) enthält. Achte beim Skimming auf:
die **Überschrift**, die **Zwischenüberschriften** und **hervorgehobene** Wörter oder Sätze, die **Bilder** und **Bildunterschriften**, den **ersten** und **letzten Satz** jedes Absatzes, **Grafiken**, **Statistiken** und die **Quelle** des Textes.

Scanning: Lesen, um nach bestimmten Informationen zu suchen

Beim **Scanning** suchst du in einem Text nach **bestimmten Informationen**, die z. B. für ein Referat wichtig sind. Dazu brauchst du nicht den gesamten Text zu lesen, sondern du suchst nach Schlüsselwörtern (**key words**) und liest nur dort genauer, wo du sie findest. Geh dabei so vor:

Schritt 1: Denk an das Schlüsselwort, nach dem du suchst, oder schreib es auf.
Schritt 2: Geh mit den Augen und dem Finger schnell durch den Text, in breiten Schlingen wie bei einem „S“ oder „Z“ oder von oben nach unten wie bei einem „U“. Dabei hast du das Schriftbild oder das Bild des Wortes, nach dem du suchst, vor Augen. Das gesuchte Wort wird dir sofort „ins Auge springen“. Lies nur dort weiter, um Näheres zu erfahren.
Schritt 3: Wenn das Schlüsselwort, nach dem du suchst, im Text nicht vorkommt, überleg dir, welche anderen Wörter mit den benötigten Informationen zu tun haben, und such nach diesen.

Finding the main ideas of a text ▸ *p. 135*

Wie finde ich die Hauptaussagen eines Textes?

① Jeder Text dreht sich um ein Thema oder hat eine Hauptaussage. Diese findest du oft im ersten Absatz. Lies ihn deshalb besonders gründlich durch.

② Die Hauptaussage wird in der Regel durch weitere Aussagen bzw. Gedanken unterstützt. Du findest sie oft im ersten oder letzten Satz der nachfolgenden Absätze.

③ Diese weiteren Aussagen bzw. Gedanken werden meist durch Beispiele und Begründungen ergänzt.

We are people too!

By Oliver Munslow (16) – 23 August 2010

① So, you think young people are different? Well, it's true! We're younger than you. But if you think that means that we don't have rights, you're wrong.

Did you know that here in Britain every citizen under 18 has important rights? For example, we all have the right to say what we think and adults should listen to us and take us seriously. And we have the right to get together with our friends in public (if we respect the rights of other people and do not break the law).

② But British children aren't taken seriously until they're 18. Too many adults think that we have nothing important to say and that we don't deserve equal rights. Here are some examples of discrimination against teenagers from my everyday life.

③ Every day I see signs on shop doors that say '2 children at a time', 'no school bags', or even 'no children unless they are with an adult'. [...]

Tipp

Die folgenden Wörter oder Wendungen werden oft im Zusammenhang mit Begründungen oder Beispielen verwendet:
and so • because • e.g. / for example • etc. • for lots of reasons • this shows that • that's why • ...

Drawing conclusions ▸ *p. 135*

Wie funktioniert schlussfolgerndes Lesen?

1. Die einfachste Form des schlussfolgernden Lesens besteht darin, die Informationen aus verschiedenen Textstellen zusammenzuführen. Bei dem Text *The Carbon Diaries 2015* (Schülerbuch, S. 35) sollst du sagen, wie *carbon rationing* Lauras Alltag verändert. Dazu musst du dir mehrere Stellen ansehen.
2. Manchmal steht die Antwort auf eine Frage nicht direkt im Text. Dann musst du sie dir erschließen. Du fragst dich z. B., ob Laura Brown und ihre Familie durch die Ausnahmesituation mehr gemeinsam unternehmen. Dafür musst du Aussagen im Text finden, die etwas mit der Frage zu tun haben:

   Lines 68–71: *My family has disappeared. Dad spends all night on his laptop, Mum is always lost on a bus somewhere and Kim just lives in her room. (...)*

   Conclusion: *The family don't spend more time together because of carbon rationing. In fact, they spend less time together.*

SPEAKING COURSE

Having a conversation ▸ *p. 138*

Ein Gespräch beginnen

Es gibt immer mehrere Möglichkeiten:

- **wenn du etwas erfragen willst** (z. B. den Weg oder die Uhrzeit): **Excuse me, do you know ... • Excuse me, can you tell me ...**
- **wenn du jemanden begrüßen möchtest oder kennenlernst: Hi. • Hello. • Good morning/evening.**
  Oft kann man das Gespräch dann mit einer allgemeinen Bemerkung weiterführen: **Great day today! • That's a great ...**
- **wenn du jemanden wiedertriffst: Hi, how are you doing? • Hi, ..., how are things? • Hi, ... Good to see/meet you.**

Ein Gespräch führen

Für den weiteren Verlauf des Gesprächs sind diese Wendungen nützlich:

- **sich vorstellen: By the way, my name's ... • I'm ... • Nice to meet you.**
- **Smalltalk machen: Have you ... before? • Have you ever ...? • Where are you from? • Do you like ...? • I like ... What about you?**
- **sich bedanken: That's great. • Thanks. / Thank you very much.**
- **sich verabschieden: See you tomorrow/next week. • Bye!**

Und wenn du etwas nicht verstanden hast, kannst du immer nachfragen:
Sorry, I didn't get that. • Sorry, could you say that again, please?

Tipp

Oft hört man zur Begrüßung auch **How are you?**
Es wird nicht erwartet, dass du darauf eine ausführliche Antwort gibst. Am besten sagst du einfach **Fine, thanks. How about you?**

Taking part in a job interview ▸ *p. 138*

Sich vorbereiten

Auf ein Vorstellungsgespräch musst du dich unbedingt vorbereiten. Du solltest Fragen zu den folgenden Bereichen beantworten können: deine Eigenschaften (**personal qualities**), Stärken (**strengths**) und Schwächen (**weaknesses**), deine Interessen (**interests**) und Arbeitserfahrungen (**work experience**), was dich an dem Jobangebot reizt (**why you're interested in the job**).

Überleg dir auch eigene Fragen, zum Beispiel zu deinem Tätigkeitsbereich (**What kind of work would I have to do?**) oder zum Tätigkeitsbeginn (**When would I have to begin?**).

Im Vorstellungsgespräch

Im Vorstellungsgespräch ist es wichtig, dass du freundlich bist und dich als positiver und interessierter Mensch präsentierst.

- **bei der Begrüßung:** Hello, nice to meet you. • Good morning.
- **warum du dich bewirbst:** I'm really interested in ... • I'm good at ..., so I think ...
- **wenn es um deine Joberfahrungen geht:** I really enjoyed working with ...
- **bei der Verabschiedung:** Goodbye and thank you very much.

Tipp
- Hör gut zu, wenn du etwas gefragt wirst.
- Sprich nicht zu viel, aber auch nicht zu wenig.
- Sprich nicht zu schnell.

Having a discussion ▸ *p. 139*

Seine Meinung zum Ausdruck bringen und erklären

1. **Expressing an opinion:** In einer Diskussion ist es gut, wenn du möglichst klar und deutlich sagst, was du zu einer bestimmten Frage denkst: I think ... • In my opinion ...
2. **Giving reasons and examples:** Genauso wichtig ist es, dass du Beispiele und Argumente nennst, die deine Meinung unterstützen – schließlich willst du deine Gesprächspartner von deinem Standpunkt überzeugen!
   because ... • First ... / Second ... / And finally ... • For example ... • Let me explain ... • That's why ...

Auf andere in einer Diskussion reagieren

1. **Asking for clarification:** Manchmal ist es notwendig nachzuhaken, weil man ein Argument nicht verstanden hat:
   Could you say that again? • Sorry, but I don't understand what you mean.
2. **Agreeing with someone:** Wenn du die Meinung eines anderen unterstützen willst, kannst du das so zum Ausdruck bringen:
   I agree (with you/...). • That's a good point. • You're right.
3. **Disagreeing with someone:** Oft widerspricht man nicht direkt, sondern leitet seine Reaktion mit Sorry, ... oder I don't think ... ein. Zeig immer Respekt für die Meinung des oder der anderen.
   I don't think you can say ... • I see what you mean, but ... • Sorry, but that's not right. • Sorry, I don't agree with you • Yes, but ...

SF Paraphrasing ▸ *p. 140*

Wie gehe ich beim *paraphrasing* vor?

- Man kann mit einem Wort umschreiben, das dieselbe Bedeutung hat: to train is the same as to practise. Oder man sagt das Gegenteil: alive is the opposite of dead
- Manchmal braucht man mehrere Wörter, z. B. wenn man etwas beschreibt oder erklärt. Dabei benutzt man ein allgemeines Wort (**general word**) und nennt weitere Eigenschaften: A racing car is a very fast car.
- Oder du umschreibst das Wort mit **... is/are like ...**: A chef is like a cook, he or she is the main cook in a restaurant.
- Du kannst auch einen Relativsatz (**relative clause**) verwenden: A garage is a place where cars are checked and repaired.
  (▸ *Mediation, WB, pp. 69–70*)

WRITING COURSE

Writing better sentences ▸ *p. 141*

Linking words

Eine Geschichte klingt interessanter, wenn du die Sätze mit **linking words** miteinander verbindest. Dabei gibt es mehrere Möglichkeiten:

- **Time phrases** wie at 7 o'clock, every morning, a few minutes later, then, next
- **Konjunktionen** wie although, because, but, so ... that, that, when, while
- **Relativpronomen** wie that und who

Adjektive und Adverbien

- Mit Adjektiven kannst du Personen, Orte oder Erlebnisse genauer und interessanter beschreiben.
  Vergleiche: The man looked into the room. ▸ The young man looked into the empty room.
- Mit Adverbien kannst du beschreiben, **wie** jemand etwas macht:
  The young man looked nervously into the empty room.

Using paragraphs ▸ *p. 141*

Structuring a text

Bei guten Texten lassen sich drei Hauptabschnitte erkennen:

- eine **Einleitung**, die in das Thema einführt
- ein **Hauptteil**, der meist aus mehreren Absätzen besteht
- ein **Schluss**, der den Text mit einer Zusammenfassung oder etwas Persönlichem zu einem interessanten Ende bringt.

Topic sentences

Am Anfang eines Absatzes sind kurze, einleitende Sätze (**topic sentences**) gut, weil sie den Lesern sofort sagen, worum es geht, z. B.

1. Orte: **My trip to ... was fantastic.** • **... is famous for ...** • **... is a great place.**
2. Personen: **... is great/funny/interesting/clever ...**
3. Aktivitäten: **... is great fun.** • **Lots of people ... every day.**

Wie kann ich meine Absätze interessant gestalten?

- Beginne mit einem interessanten Einstiegssatz: **You'll never guess what happened to me today!** • **Did I tell you that ...?**
- Fange für jeden neuen Aspekt einen neuen Absatz an.
- Beende deinen Text mit einer Zusammenfassung oder etwas Persönlichem.

Writing a report – collecting and organizing ideas ▸ *p. 142*

Worauf kommt es bei einem Bericht an?

- Gib dem Leser **eine schnelle Orientierung**, was passiert ist.
- Beginne mit **wichtigen Informationen** und gib erst dann Detailinformationen.
- Ein Bericht gibt immer Antworten auf die **5 Ws**:
  Who? What? When? Where? Why? und manchmal auch auf **How?**
- Verwende das **simple past**.

Correcting your text ▸ *p. 142*

Spelling mistakes

Tipp

- Manche Wörter haben Buchstaben, die man nicht spricht, aber schreibt, z. B. **knife**, **climb**.
- Manchmal ändert sich die Schreibweise, wenn ein Wort eine Endung erhält, z. B. **take** → **taking**, **terrible** → **terribly**, **lucky** → **luckily**, **try** → **tries** (**aber stay** → **stays**), **run** → **running**, **drop** → **dropped**.
- Beim Plural tritt manchmal noch ein **-e** zum **-s**, z. B. **church** → **churches**.

tomato [tə'mɑːtəʊ], *pl* **tomatoes** Tomate

wife [waɪf], *pl* **wives** [waɪvz] Ehefrau

drop (-**pp**-) [drɒp] fallen lassen

forget (-**tt**-) [fə'get] vergessen

Grammar mistakes

Tipp

- Im **simple present** wird in der 3. Person Singular **-s** angehängt: **she knows**
- **Unregelmäßige Verben:** Manche Verben bilden die Formen des *simple past* und des Partizip Perfekt *(past participle)* unregelmäßig. Die unregelmäßigen Formen musst du lernen. Die Liste steht auf S. 215–216.
  go – went – gone; buy – bought – bought
- **Verneinung bei Vollverben:** Im *simple present* mit ***don't/doesn't***, im *simp le past* mit **didn't**, z. B. **He doesn't speak French, he didn't learn it at school**.
- **Satzstellung**: Im Englischen gilt immer (auch im Nebensatz):
  a) subject – verb – object (S-V-O) **... when I saw my brother.**
  ... als ich meinen Bruder sah.
  b) Orts- vor Zeitangabe **I bought a nice book in town yesterday. Ich habe gestern in der Stadt ein schönes Buch gekauft.**

MEDIATION SKILLS

SF Mediation ▸ *p. 147*

Worauf muss ich bei *mediation* achten?

- Übersetze nicht alles wörtlich.
- Gib nur das Wesentliche weiter. Oft gibt dir die Fragestellung Hinweise, worauf es ankommt.
- Verwende kurze und einfache Sätze.
- Wenn du ein Wort nicht kennst, umschreibe es oder ersetze es durch ein anderes Wort.

Was kann ich tun, wenn ich ein wichtiges Wort nicht kenne?

Vielleicht findest du es manchmal schwer, mündliche Aussagen oder schriftliche Textvorlagen in die andere Sprache zu übertragen, z. B. weil dein Wortschatz nicht ausreicht, dir bekannte Wörter im Augenblick nicht einfallen, spezielle Fachbegriffe auftauchen. Manche Wörter kannst du umschreiben, z. B. mithilfe von Relativsätzen wie:

It's somebody/a person who ... • It's something that you use to ... • It's an animal that ... • It's a place where ...

GF 3 Talking about the present ► *p. 152*

3.1 The simple present

Dave Wilson **usually** gets the bus to school.
On Mondays his mother takes him in the car.
He **never** cycles to school because it's too far.

Das ***simple present*** wird verwendet,

◄ um über Handlungen und Ereignisse zu sprechen, die **wiederholt, regelmäßig, immer** oder **nie** geschehen (oft mit Zeitangaben wie *always, never, usually, sometimes, often, every week, on Mondays* usw.).

Dave and his family live in Manchester.
He plays hockey and collects models of old cars.
His dad works for a building company.

◄ um über **Dauerzustände**, **Hobbys** und **Berufe** zu sprechen.

! *He, she, it* – das „s" muss mit.

Verneinte Sätze	I don't cycle to school.	Dave doesn't walk to school.
Fragen	Do you go to school by bus? **Where** do the Wilsons live?	Does your mother take you in the car? **When** does Dave's mother take him in the car?

3.2 The present progressive

What's Dave doing? –
Just now he's cleaning his bike.

Dave (on the phone) I can't talk right now, Jack. I'm cleaning my bike.

This week Dave's grandma is staying at the Wilsons' because Dave's mum is ill.

Das ***present progressive*** wird verwendet,

◄ um über Handlungen und Ereignisse zu sprechen, die **jetzt gerade im Gange** sind (oft mit Angaben wie *at the moment, now, just*).

! Die Handlung, um die es geht, kann für einen Augenblick unterbrochen sein, z. B. durch ein Telefonat. Wichtig ist, dass sie noch nicht abgeschlossen ist.

◄ um über **vorübergehende Zustände** zu sprechen (begrenzter Zeitraum: *this week*).

Verneinte Sätze	The Wilsons aren't working.	Dave isn't watching TV.
Fragen	Are you watching TV? **What** are you doing?	Is Dave cleaning his bike? **Who** is Dave talking to?

GF 4 Talking about the past ► *p. 153–154*

4.1 The simple past

Last Friday Katie's family flew to Spain.
Letzten Freitag ist Katies Familie nach Spanien geflogen / flog Katies Familie nach Spanien.
Two years ago the Websters moved to Bath.
Vor zwei Jahren sind die Websters nach Bath gezogen.

Wenn man über Vergangenes berichtet – zum Beispiel, wenn man etwas erzählt –, benutzt man überwiegend das ***simple past***. Man beschreibt damit Handlungen, Ereignisse und Zustände, die zu einer bestimmten Zeit in der Vergangenheit *(yesterday, last Friday, two years ago, in 2003, between 2005 and 2008, ...)* stattfanden.

Verneinte Sätze	They didn't fly to France.	Katie didn't want to go at first.
Fragen	Did you go on holiday last year? **Where** did you go?	Did Katie like it? **When** did the Websters move to Bath?

4.2 The past progressive

What were you doing yesterday at 3.30? –
I was waiting for my sister at the school doors. She was still talking to our Maths teacher.

Das ***past progressive*** wird verwendet,

◄ um über Handlungen und Ereignisse zu sprechen, die zu einer bestimmten Zeit in der Vergangenheit noch im Gange, also noch nicht abgeschlossen waren.

Angela was just crossing the road when she saw her boyfriend.
Angela war gerade dabei, die Straße zu überqueren, ...

◄ wenn man beschreiben will, was gerade vor sich ging *(she was just crossing the road)*, als etwas anderes passierte *(she saw her boyfriend)*.

Verneinte Sätze	You weren't listening.	It wasn't snowing when we left the house.
Fragen	Were you watching TV? **What** were they doing?	Was she crossing the road when it happened? **What** was she doing?

4.4 The present perfect

Will Smith is great. I've seen most of his films.
Luke has **already** done his Maths homework, but he hasn't started his French **yet**.
Have you **ever** been to Paris?
– No, I haven't. But I've **always** wanted to go.

Mel has lost her mobile. Her dad is very angry.

! Das ***present perfect*** hat mit der **Vergangenheit <u>und</u> mit der Gegenwart** zu tun. Es wird verwendet,

◄ wenn man sagen will, **dass** jemand etwas getan hat oder **dass** etwas geschehen ist. Dabei ist nicht wichtig, wann es geschehen ist – ein genauer Zeitpunkt wird nicht genannt. Das *present perfect* steht oft mit Adverbien der <u>unbestimmten</u> Zeit wie *already, just, never, ever, not ... yet*.
Oft hat die Handlung Auswirkungen auf die Gegenwart (Mels Vater ist wütend, weil sie ihr Handy verloren hat).

We've lived in Berlin **since April.**
Wir wohnen <u>seit April</u> in Berlin.

since+Zeitpunkt

We've lived in Berlin **for three months.**
Wir wohnen <u>seit drei Monaten</u> in Berlin.

for+Zeitraum

◄ für **Zustände**, die in der Vergangenheit begonnen haben und jetzt noch andauern (oft mit ***since*** bzw. ***for***).

! Im Deutschen steht in diesen Fällen meist das Präsens, im Englischen <u>muss</u> das *present perfect* stehen.

Verneinte Sätze	I haven't been to Paris yet.	Luke hasn't done his French homework.
Fragen	Have you been to Paris? **What** have you done?	Has Mel found her mobile yet? **Which** of these films have you seen already?

GF 5 Talking about the future ► *p. 155*

5.1 The *going to*-future

My boyfriend says he's going to be an engineer.
Mein Freund sagt, er will Ingenieur werden.
Look at those clouds. There's going to be a storm.
... Es wird ein Gewitter geben.

Das **Futur mit *going to*** wird verwendet,

◄ wenn man über **Vorhaben, Pläne, Absichten** für die Zukunft sprechen will.

◄ um auszudrücken, dass etwas **wahrscheinlich gleich geschehen wird** – es gibt bereits deutliche **Anzeichen** dafür (*hier:* die Wolken am Himmel).

5.2 The *will*-future

It will be cold and windy, and we will get some rain in the afternoon.
I'll be 15 next October.
I expect Ella will be late again as usual.
Ich nehme an, Ella kommt wie üblich wieder zu spät.
Just a moment. I'll open the door for you.
Moment. Ich mache Ihnen die Tür auf.
I won't tell anyone what's happened. I promise.
Ich sage niemandem, was passiert ist. ...

Das **Futur mit *will*** wird verwendet,

◄ um **Vorhersagen** über die Zukunft zu äußern.
Oft geht es dabei um Dinge, die man nicht beeinflussen kann, z.B. das Wetter.

◄ um eine **Vermutung** auszudrücken (oft eingeleitet mit *I think, I'm sure, I expect, maybe*).

◄ wenn man sich **spontan** – also ohne es im Voraus geplant zu haben – zu etwas **entschließt**. Oft geht es dabei um **Hilfsangebote** oder **Versprechen**.

5.3 The present progressive (future meaning)

We're driving to Scotland next Friday to visit my grandparents.
I'm meeting a friend in town tonight.

Das ***present progressive*** wird verwendet, wenn etwas **für die Zukunft fest geplant** oder **fest verabredet** ist (manchmal spricht man vom *diary future*). Durch eine Zeitangabe wie *tonight* oder aus dem Zusammenhang muss klar sein, dass es um etwas Zukünftiges geht.

1 LISTENING Friends on the net
Richard B; Angie A; Robin D; Lisa C; Josie E

2 LISTENING Voicemail messages
1 T; *2* F; *3* N; *4* F; *5* T; *6* T; *7* T; *8* F; *9* F; *10* T; *11* N; *12* F

3 LISTENING Talking about free time
1 hip-hop *2* four thirty/4.30 *3* twenty-five/25 *4* grandmother *5* five thirty/5.30 *6* mum/mother *7* tennis *8* cricket *9* water *10* swimming/to the swimming club *11* Monday *12* 4.54

4 SPEAKING Dumped
1 has been dumped by a friend or boyfriend
2 surprised/shocked/upset by text message, doesn't understand what has happened, probably feeling hurt, unhappy
3 talk to a good friend, go out with others, join a club and meet new people, do hobbies
4 **No** – text message not a good way to end a relationship, a person who gets dumped by text message maybe feels that he/she was not very important to the partner
Yes – quick and easy way to end a relationship, no arguments, no hard words, no long explanation, no difficult situation, no crying, etc., breaking up always hurts, so it doesn't matter how you do it

5 SPEAKING A cartoon
The cartoon shows a father talking to his teenage son, who is standing next to him. The father doesn't look very happy. He doesn't know what blogging is, so he tells his son to stop it because he imagines it's something bad. The boy maybe thinks his father is strict without reason, and old-fashioned
The cartoon's message is that older people often don't know and don't trust modern electronic communication.
This can make understanding between parents and teenagers difficult. I (don't) agree with the cartoon artist because …

6 SPEAKING Comparing photos
Picture 1 shows a family of four (parents, son, daughter) on holiday in a sunny place. There is a swimming pool in the background. The four people are sitting at a table next to the pool. There are cakes, ice cream and soft drinks on the table. The atmosphere is relaxed.
Picture 2 shows three young people, two girls and a boy, who are sightseeing in London without family. They are looking at a guide book, maybe they are talking about where to go next

Holidays with parents
Advantages: they organize, plan, pay and drive, you can count on them if you need help or if there are problems, you can relax and not worry about planning, money, safety
Disadvantages: you may miss friends of your own age, you may have to do things that you are not very interested in, you may have to get up earlier than you hoped, you may argue
Holidays with friends
Advantages: you can plan everything yourselves, you can do things that interest teenagers, it's fun being with good friends, you can stay up late, you can travel with just a rucksack, you can stay at youth hostels, it's good experience to be alone and do things for yourself, you have to be organized, careful and look after all your things yourself
Disadvantages: there are no parents to help, pay, plan, drive or rent a car, you have to fit in with the rest of the group, it may not be easy being together with the same people every day, you may argue because each of you wants something different

7 WRITING A questionnaire (Individual answers)

8 WRITING A picture story
Anna's boyfriend dumped her by text message. Did he have a new girlfriend now? She was crying when she phoned her best friend. The friend advised Anna not to sit at home. Anna decided to visit her cousin at the weekend. She would go on her moped the next day. When she left home on her moped, it was raining. An hour later she stopped at a café on the way. A nice young guy came in. He sat at the next table. They chatted for half an hour and they laughed. They liked each other.They left the café together. They would meet again the next day. Had Anna forgotten her old boyfriend already?

9, 10 WRITING What's your opinion? A report
(Individual answers)

11 MEDIATION A letter to a problem page
Was man tun soll:
eine neue Freundschaft suchen, alles loswerden, was an die Beziehung erinnert – E-mails, Fotos usw., sich mit irgendetwas beschäftigen, damit man abgelenkt ist, erst zu Bett gehen, wenn man sehr müde ist, Dinge unternehmen, für die man früher keine Zeit hatte, mit Freunden/-innen über die Situation reden.
Was man nicht tun soll:
romantische Musik spielen, romantische Filme anschauen oder glücklichen Paaren zuschauen, Plätze aufsuchen, die Erinnerungen an die glückliche Zeit wachrufen.

12 MEDIATION A film
The film *Crazy* is about Benny who is disabled. He often changes schools because his grades are not good. His parents send him to a boarding school, not his first. He has problems making friends, but his room mate Janosch becomes his friend. Janosch likes fun and girls more than school. All is fine until they both fancy the same girl, Malen. So the friends have a problem. It's a film about growing up, friendship and love.

13 READING Daniel's blog
b) *1* C; *2* C; *3* C; *4* B; *5* B
c) *1* T; *2* F; *3* N; *4* F; *5* T; *6* T; *7* T; *8* N; *9* F; *10* T
d) *1* Maria: Spain; Sven: Sweden; Nina: Great Britain; Jean-Paul: France; Max: Germany; Elena: Greece; Anna: Poland
2 Daniel liked: his tennis and English course, the accommodation in college, the international atmosphere, the English breakfast, the conversation group, the Oxford city bus tour.
3 Daniel didn't like: having to be in his room by 10.30 pm, the discussion on tennis tactics, strategy and mental attitude, the video analysis of how each student played.

14 USE OF LANGUAGE A first date
a) have changed – went – advice – who – doing – by – to stand – carefully – about – with – relaxed – yourself – tell – than – well
b) *1* D; *2* C; *3* A; *4* E; *5* B, *6* G
c) *1* wear; *2* movie; *3* opinion; *4* role
d) *1* same; *2* enjoy; *3* boring; *4* late